PUBLISHED IN JUNE 2017

THE TITLE, STYLE OF MAKE-UP AND
ALMANACK ARE STRICTLY

Foulsham's Or

OLD MOO
ALMANACK

697   THE ORIGINAL COPYRIGHT EDITION   **2018**

2018 – The Year for
Optimistic Rebuilding

am designating 2018 as the year for Optimistic Rebuilding because of two powerful
influences. The first is a change in the influence of Pluto which brought us the great financial
crisis of 2008 and subsequent disruption. Pluto will begin its departure from us and this
provides great easement. The second is that Saturn enters its own sign, Capricorn. This will
focus its influences on much more practicality. Both modifications will change minds and
promote practical rebuilding.

These optimistic feelings will begin in an On–Off pattern initially, but will settle over us
permanently in 2018 and last until 2025. We may well feel ourselves lucky in this, as we
watch the traumas of government in the USA and Europe. This change in our circumstances
is brought to us by the influences of Uranus in Taurus. Uranus doesn't lose its revolutionary
purpose, but in Taurus it induces technological innovations and I expect exciting
announcements in medicine and helpful robotics.

Though we are breaking out to a much brighter future, we have yet to resolve the crisis
of 2008. Since before 2000, I warned that the planetary influences were virtually the same
as those which produced the financial crash of 1929. We were breaking good fiscal rules
and sleep-walking towards a collapse. Well, 2008 produced the collapse and it revealed the
corruption that I predicted. It was seen all over the financial Industry and the complicity of
Governments was clear. Yet still, we haven't had the crash that must be its rightful conclusion.

© **2017 by OLD MOORE PUBLICATIONS**
Published under Annual Licence by W. Foulsham & Co. Ltd
Printed and bound by CPI Group (UK) Ltd, Croydon, CR0 4YY
News trade distribution by Seymour 020 7429 4000

Tel: (01628) 400631
The Old Barrel Store,
Drayman's Lane,
Marlow, Bucks SL7 2FF

This matter will be addressed in 2018. Reality must be faced because every beginning need its appropriate ending. The trigger will be Pluto moving through Capricorn. Then Uranus wi insist that all the corrections are made and everything be put back – *very differently*. Culpri will stand exposed, in printing so much new money that currencies have been junked. The will be seen to have exhausted all trust in their prudent management. Uranus will insist o modernising *everything* and it will want to leave behind radical changes to our financial system.

Uranus has so often been the breaker of venerable traditions that I must now conside crypto currency as part of the solution it may apply. Explaining crypto currency is well abov my pay grade, but it is new, 'super-geek' thinking that has produced a concept for digit currency that is now widely accepted by Internet Corporations. Crypto currency, as the nex big digital spoiler in the financial world, could be Uranus's preferred tool.

BitCoin is the longest traded and strongest of these currencies. The Establishment hasn yet been able to accept the whole phenomenon, and this too becomes another reason t expect it to be forced into play. Uranus will see it as bright, shiny disruption.

To re-establish financial stability, we need a system that cannot be abused by deceitfu profiteers. Crypto currencies have been designed to meet such needs, so Bitcoin can't b manipulated by bankers, financiers, or governments. Uranus will almost certainly want to mi a financial revolution that puts *digital* at the heart of a new and democratic financial solution

Much more is also brewing. Now I see whole populations becoming increasingly *spiritual* Instead of belonging to established religions, people have to look within *themselves* to finc personal spirituality. I expect this movement to percolate across to politics. If I replace the word *spirituality* with *humanity*, you may see how it could drift. Astrology explains that human being are naturally collective and inclusive. Too many politicians are insensitive to this. The nev movement towards humanity will spread amongst young intelligentsia on social media and I se new political groupings born in this. The political classes will be wrong footed in this evolution because often, they won't be looking in the right direction. I believe these ideas may gain mor traction from a major corruption scandal at the end of the year that will have global significance

Looking at Europe I continue to wait for the corrections that so obviously need to b made. The Bank of Europe's treatment of its poorer members reveals the uncaring corruptior of this financial institution and European politics. Its treatment of the Greek debt problem i indefensible. It used the tactics of a back-street money lender to impose self-serving condition that were known to be distressing. Today, the Greek people are suffering greatly at its hand The EU is permanently manipulated by unelected representatives with no concern for it population. I expect to see more populism produce further exits from the group in 2018.

You have my very best wishes through 2018 and I urge you to make your own contributior to our future. Put your ideas into practice.

Dr Francis Moore, September 2016

1 to 9

Numbers and Their Amazing Effect on Luck

you can count from 1 to 9 you can use this book! 'All luck revolves round numbers!', declares J. deVille, author. Each hour, day and date is overned by one of the nine numbers, be it the 9th or the 27th. Why will something be successful one day, but not the next? 'Because f numbers!' he says. 'When the wrong number is chosen – which is sually the case – the chances of success are only 1 in 9', he opines. 'You e usually therefore more likely to fail 9 times out of 10 – but that ratio an be turned on its head!' he declares.

'THE DIFFERENCE BETWEEN A SUCCESSFUL SURGICAL OPERATION ND A FAILURE', he believes, 'COULD ALL BE DOWN TO THE HOUR AND HE DATE!'

Of course, dates are given to us over which we have no control – the uthor shows how to circumvent this problem.

'Numbers are more vital than astrology, biorhythms and other cyclic rocesses', he claims. 'They dominate our lives and most of us never now it.' The author's first address was at No. 7; he began primary school n the 7th and entered college on the 25th (2+5=7); got married on the 4th (twice 7); and so on – 'and yet if I use 7 to bring me luck it won't york. So-called "lucky numbers" are another matter altogether!'

He continues: 'If you have not been lucky it may be because you have ot done things at the right time, not because you are a fool.'

'I will show you once and for all what your propitious numbers could e – and not what you think they are!'

No rituals required! No visualisation or applied concentration! You eed only to be able to count from 1 to 9 (numbers above that are relevant). We are restricted to what claims can be made for this book, ut we can cite a few of its chapter headings: The Luck & Significance f Numbers; Improving Business; Successful Interviews; The Woman Who ound Herself A Husband; Names & Places Have Numbers; The Man Who ived Off Gambling; Cycles.

To receive the book '1 to 9: Numbers & Their Amazing Effect On Luck', lease send **£9.99** cheque or postal order, payable to 'Finbarr', to: inbarr, Folkestone CT20 2QQ. Overseas send £15.99 to cover air mail. Major cards accepted, please give number, start date, expiry date & last three digits or security number on back of card. If in a hurry please dd 80p & write 'PRIORITY' on face of envelope for extra fast delivery. Catalogue of unusual books 95p. PLEASE DON'T FORGET TO GIVE YOUR JAME AND ADDRESS!

DEFEATING DEPRESSION

5 words changed my life!' claims author Deborah Anderson. 20 years f depression lifted! Not a prayer, not a chant. Information here not ound elsewhere. Essential reading for those who have tried the usual reatments and failed. £9.99 from: **Finbarr (OD), Folkestone, Kent** .T20 2QQ. Overseas £14.99.

NEW SALT MAGIC RITES

Chapters include: **Salt Magic Brings Money – Influencing Another Person's Thoughts & Actions – Salt Rites to Protect Against Physical Injury – Salt Rite To Get A Job.** Are you aware that sprinkling salt outside your front door could keep unwanted persons away? Everything is explained in this volume! Also details for sprinkling salt on important documents and lottery coupons. Common salt from your supermarket is all you need. Note these unsolicited testimonials (copies of originals available on request): 'Have already had two wins on the pools' (M.B., Fleetwood): 'In ten minutes my violent son quietened down ... have had no trouble from him since' (P.E., Manchester): 'IT REALLY WORKS! I won £1411' (A.P., Grimsby); 'Since I got your book ... money has come into my home in different ways ... my son has paid off his debts ... I bless the day I sent for this book (D.L., Hove) – this same lady wrote again five months later: 'The salt rites are still working for us ... every day we receive something good!' To receive 'New Salt Magic Rites' please send £9.99 to: Finbarr (OS), Folkestone, Kent CT20 2QQ (address complete) Overseas send £14.99.

Lost Magick Rites

From the Archives of Finbarr

Winning Court Cases!

Getting Someone Out Of Your Life!

Bringing Back Someone!

Magick rites from long out-of-print books by Marcus Bottomley and Frank Gupta, copyright Finbarr, made available in one volume!

In response to demand from serious collectors of magical lore we are publishing this work of *authentic magick rites*.

Magick rites that allegedly influence the outcome of court hearings! Magick rites which, allegedly, sway witnesses and judges! 'With magick, a case is won before the parties even appear in court', claims author.

Magick rites which allegedly *compel* another to leave! Magick rites which allegedly can break up another's love affair.

Magick rites which shield and protect the magician from harm.

This is the only book to contain these particularly rare and sought after rites!

There's a magick rite here which allegedly cures male impotency.

A magick rite for allegedly uncovering the identity of a thief.

A magick rite for allegedly punishing an enemy.

Magick rites which allegedly make an estranged lover contact you, or return.

A magick rite for allegedly identifying the person one will marry.

Magick rites which allegedly place another under one's control.

Magick rites which allegedly control the forces of luck, influencing the outcome of gambling; increasing one's fortune in business.

Magick rites which allegedly sever a relationship.

Magick rites which allegedly enables one to find a job/promotion.

Magick rites which allegedly influence employers.

A magick rite which reverses curses; restoring good fortune.

A magick rite which allegedly controls ghosts and malicious spirits.

These are the magick rites we have been asked time and again to publish, for the benefit of all collectors of magickal lore.

Magick rites which allegedly increase mental powers, improving concentration and memory.

Aphrodisiac magick! – Magick for acquiring riches! – Magick for peace and harmony in the home! – Voodoo money, luck and subjugation spells!

For the serious collector, this is a goldmine of rare and closely guarded folk magick; only Finbarr holds the copyright. Despite the potency attached to these rites some are remarkably easy to do.

Strange powers are attributed to these magick rites.

These rites have been passed by word of mouth, generation to generation under oaths of secrecy, through the long passages of time. Only Finbarr possesses their printed copyright.

These are the magick rites used by professional occultists who, for substantial fees, offer their services to those in need.

These magick rites allegedly give the reader/practitioner strange powers over circumstances and people. According to the authors this is 'real' magick: not dependent on visualization or positive thinking.

'Science cannot explain it and never will', they say.

To receive LOST MAGICK RITES FROM THE ARCHIVES OF FINBARR please send £9.99 to: Finbarr (OL), Folkestone, CT20 2QQ. Overseas £15.99.

2018 – World Preview

The international climate ricochets from month to month as the planets alternate from relaxed to challenging alignments and back. On four occasions – 2 January, 28 May, 13 July and 6 August – the planets form a 'kite' formation, a rare combination of hard and soft aspects. Kite patterns are very exciting because they provide positive indications of the periods when people can succeed by turning their plans into practical reality. The most dangerous period of the year centres on the eclipsed Full Moon in Virgo on 2 March. A tense and muddled 'T Square' between the Sun, Moon, Mars and Neptune indicates the risk of wars born of confusion. My strong advice is that governments should keep back-channels wide open to avoid accidents.

THE ECONOMY

The planets which are most closely related to economic cycles are Jupiter, which indicates growth, hope and inflation, and Saturn, which rules austerity, fear and contraction. Both are necessary for a balanced economy. Jupiter is weak in Scorpio for most of the year so we should expect low growth and low inflation. When Jupiter enters Sagittarius in mid November the mood will shift and I see signs of a take-off in some sectors, particularly those related to transport and aerospace. US commerce will lead the emerging boom. Saturn is strong in Capricorn indicating the restructuring of old industries and the creation of new infrastructure to support new build, which is the basis of their future prosperity. There are no major aspects between the two planets in 2018 so we should not expect any sudden upsurge or downward surge. Jupiter's prolonged trine to Neptune brings a risk of speculative bubbles so if an investment looks too good, it probably is! Be particularly cautious this year.

THE UNITED KINGDOM

Readers will be aware that in previous issues I advised against leaving the EU. When the stars are in a volatile phase, there is a need to promote stability on the ground and in politics. Our surprising and most unlikely referendum has sent me back to appraise my earlier writings. It still seems clear that negotiations will be very complex, protracted and that they will require more compromise from the UK than 'Leave' supporters would wish. The volatility of the situation is indicated by Pluto's square to the UK's Moon, a position all astrologers recognise will bring very deep, profound change. July is our most intense month. A snap referendum on plans for a Scottish secession are in the frame, and the prospects of the Scottish Nationalists winning are greater than they were at the last attempt. It will become apparent that most voters just want a period of calm and stability but this is unlikely to be their experience for much of the year.

EUROPE

Speculation on the break-up of the European Union is set to continue with little respite. The EU's founding horoscope is under higher than average pressure, but no more so than one would normally expect in an institution which has always lived from one crisis to another. However, a deeper, long-term story is told by the 'progressed' horoscope, which has a dangerous Moon–Mars conjunction in January. This is the strongest possible indication of conflict and break-up. There is a high chance of far-right conflicts targeting refugees, but the main story looks like being that at least one other country may follow the UK out of the Union. No prediction is 100% secure, but the Union will require all the assistance it can get from global financial institutions if the poorer countries are to be able to remain.

THE USA

The USA is under a negative phase represented by Saturn's opposition to the Sun. The economy, corporations and institutions are resilient, but the government will be constantly hit by reality checks. While Saturn is retrograde from April to September the country will be dominated by nostalgia. The next three years are reflected by the chart for 20 January 2017, the day of the inauguration of Donald Trump. This took place under a highly stressful 'T Square' between Jupiter, Uranus and Pluto. This coincided with the revolutionary mood which brought Trump to power. But, because it is present in his inauguration chart, it tells us about his entire presidency. It is likely that his term in office will be dominated by conflict. At the very moment that Trump became President, the Moon in Scorpio was in a trine with a conjunction of Venus, Mars and Neptune in Pisces. This indicates a high possibility of fraud in government though it seems more likely accidental than deliberate. It will be caused by the careless management of the boundaries between business and politics. I am looking for a major international scandal in December that could fit this bill. If Trump fulfills this prophecy, even a replacement President would be handicapped.

RUSSIA

Like the USA, Russia is under a significant Saturn transit to its Sun, but with reverse effect. The Sun is in Capricorn, Saturn's own sign. Though it appears to be under greater pressure, the government will be even more stable. For example, there are some indications of democratic pressure in July but public opinion, ruled by the Moon in Virgo's harmonious trine to the Sun, will support the government.

CHINA

China shares the same Saturn aspect as the USA and Russia. It is in an easier aspect than the USA's but not as relaxed as Russia's. So, China remains generally strong and countries who attempt to challenge it economically or strategically will come off the worse for their efforts.

Donald Trump

© PA Images

'People may not always think big themselves, but the can still get very excited by those who do. People wan to believe that something is the biggest and the greates and the most spectacular.' These are Donald J. Trump own words in his book *The Art of the Deal,* and he' certainly the *biggest* these days! Since inheriting hi family's real estate and construction company, throug his involvement with beauty contests and a US realit television series, *The Apprentice*, he's assumed the to executive spot of all: 45th President of the Unite States. It's been quite a ride, Trump's appearance i US politics has been colourful and controversial to sa the least, invoking much ire from both Democrats an Republicans. Can he survive this wealth of opposition

Donald John Trump was born on 14 June 1946, giving him Sun in curious Gemini Moon in optimistic Sagittarius and proud, flamboyant Leo rising close to fiery Mars. Here is a combative, yet skilled and unabashed self-promoter. With that Moon in forward-looking Sagittarius he has no time for introversion; this is a 'can do' type who is always or the move and is impatient with whatever might slow him down. His birth chart as a whole gives him a tremendous capacity to invent life as he goes along.

With the Sun in conjunction to Uranus, President Trump likes to make his presence felt by shocking others. Sun conjoined with wilful, erratic Uranus in Gemini produces the unconventional 'one-off', the offbeat, unpredictable type. His Moon also opposes Uranus making him prone to impulse and sudden changes of mind, but Venus in emotional and traditional Cancer underlies this with a deep sensitivity hidden behind a tough, defensive exterior which is the result of a harsh link to staid Saturn.

In December 2017, Trump may be having serious thoughts about his life, career and future. This month could easily mark a time when he will give up trying to run the show himself and start to rely entirely on the efforts of his team. Having said that, the main planetary influence for President Trump is the Jupiter effect, which is associated with personal growth and luck. But this doesn't mean it won't also be a bumpy ride as he encounters limitations, and opposition to his ideas and plans. The 'progressed' moon in contact with power-driven Pluto indicates a major conflict that may undermine his position as Commander in Chief. By April, cracks may be appearing and he may now suffer major defeat at the hands of political opponents. If he survives this period, he may not go on past April 2018 because even harder aspects in his progressed chart will become evident.

9

Prince Harry

© PA Images

Prince Harry, the younger son of Prince Charles and the late Princess Diana, is one of the most popular members of the British Royal family – and with good reason. He was born on 15 September 1984 at 4.20 pm which makes him a Sun-sign Virgo, though his birth chart as a whole is quite unique. It reveals him to be physically adventurous and brave but also demonstrates a truly sensitive side which, as he grows older, is now beginning to reveal itself. Mercury also in Virgo gives him good powers of communication, both verbal and written, whilst Capricorn on his Ascendant strengthens his physique but also generates a really private Harry that few people get to see.

There has been much talk recently about Prince Harry's willingness to speak out on mental health issues and indeed about the trauma he has personally suffered as a result of the premature loss of his mother. With several of his planets in Sagittarius, Harry is a tireless campaigner and he has the ability to turn his own past problems into tools he can use to assist others. One would have to go a long way to discover a more generally 'rounded' chart that that of Prince Harry but it is just possible there will be problems ahead when the outspoken side of his nature makes a periodic appearance.

In relationships, Prince Harry plays his cards close to his chest. He is presently being linked with the actress Meghan Markle. Old Moore cannot determine at this time whether Meghan will become Harry's life partner but his progressed chart does show a period in the spring of 2018 when Venus is especially well aspected and if he were to choose to make an annoucement about his personal future, this would be a likely time.

In the very near future Prince Harry will be searching for something new and demanding to do with his life. Everything about his birth chart shows him to be a peerless ambassador for his country and his family and he may soon take on a very official role possibly related to the British Commonwealth or the UN. It is highly likely that he will serve a term as a Governor General, most likely of Australia.

One feature that has not shown in Prince Harry's life before now is his undoubted skill as a writer. His strong Virgoan traits and his progressed chart show how important the written word will become to him in the longer-term future. Harry remains a very physically motivated individual but needs to be careful regarding physical mishaps later in 2018, perhaps somehow related to animals. When the time comes, Prince Harry will make an excellent parent and we can expect him to continue to enjoy his popularity in the decades ahead.

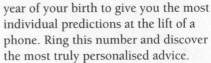

11

Theresa May

© PA Images

Six years have passed since Old Moore predicted that Theresa May might one day become Britain's Prime Minister which, as we now know, has turned out to be the case. At the time of writing, she is holding the steady course in Number 10 that we might expect from someone who enjoys four of her most significant planets in the Fire sign of Leo. Theresa was born on 1 October 1956, which puts her Sun in compliant Libra – a sure indication that she is capable of seeing another person's point of view, even if all the Fire in her chart also fits her for the many battles that life in Westminster demands. After receiving a good education and working for some time in the Bank of England, she entered politics as a Conservative MP in 1997 and enjoyed almost instant success in the ministerial roles to which she was appointed.

Theresa May is a no-nonsense individual. She doesn't suffer fools gladly but has an astrological brake that prevents all that Leo from making her too outspoken. Little Mercury and giant Jupiter were both in Virgo when she was born and this makes her extremely careful regarding her public image. She will not willingly become involved in any argument she fears she might lose and is a careful and calculating person. The scandals that tend to attach themselves to some politicians are not likely to touch Theresa May.

As Old Moore writes these words a general election has been called for June 2017 and Theresa's progressed birth chart for the time of the announcement suggests that this was good timing. Theresa is no natural gambler, though once committed to a course of action she will see it through to the bitter end. She will not be rushed or pushed, takes little notice of criticism she considers to be without justification but at the same time retains a certain 'common touch'.

Old Moore sees Theresa May loosening her grip on being in control of the very centre of British politics. Because of a certain natural reserve, together with the slightly imperious tendencies bestowed by Leo, it is unlikely that she will be universally loved but will be deeply respected, even by those who disagree vehemently with her point of view. If ever there was a character who has all the necessary attributes to see Great Britain through Brexit and to achieve the seemingly impossible on the way, that person is likely to be the unflappable Theresa May. But there are huge bumps on the road that lies before her.

The Only Prayer You Will Ever Need

A PRAYER LIKE NO OTHER – *A PRAYER WITHOUT WORDS*

Elvira Powel writes:

I received this prayer from my uncle who was on his deathbed. I will never forget his words, 'This is the only prayer you will ever need.'

It changed my life.

I was out of a job. I had lost my home. My health was failing

Yet this prayer changed everything.

It is worth more to me than anything money can buy, for I know that whatever I need it can supply.

It brought me hope. It even made my children better behaved!

I have always believed in prayer. But my prayers were not always answered. None of this matters now, for I now have the only prayer I will ever need.

My long night of darkness was over. Into the light I emerged and not only were problems solved but my life was at last going forward.

I found a job I love, one that is secure. And I met a wonderful man: a successful businessman who loves not only me but my children too.

I put all this down to this one prayer.

When my uncle explained it to me I was amazed. 'How can a prayer be without words?' I asked. 'Don't question it', he replied, 'just do it.'

He said, 'Even if one doesn't believe in the God of the Church it will work for you. *Just do it!*'

I had never known anything like it.

It takes only moments and can be used by anyone of any faith or religion.

And it has inspired me to write this book. The publisher tried this prayer and tells me that he now uses it every day. 'I will not argue with what your uncle said, "the only prayer you will ever need". I am amazed by it and the immediate help it has given me for many situations.'

Whatever your need, use this prayer.

If you need more money, use this prayer.

If you need to solve an intractable problem, use this prayer.

If you need love, use this prayer.

If you want someone to love you again, this is the only prayer you need.

If you are ill, trust in this prayer, for your health is about to change.

My sister's life was a misery on account of so many allergies. This prayer changed everything. Now she enjoys life to the full.

I explained it to a young colleague who was anxious about her next driving test. She passed after using the prayer (she had failed the previous 7 times).

I could go on.

If anyone had told me previously that I could use or 'say' a prayer in which no words were spoken I would not have believed.

But because it was my uncle who told me, and I had always trusted him completely, I took his word for it.

I am so excited that I feel the whole world should know about it. I can't see why it should be kept hidden.

It is the best thing to ever happen to me. I now live in faith, for I have this prayer which unfailingly helps and guides me.

I use it daily to ensure that my day goes well. And so it does. I believe I am living a 'charmed life'; and I am so grateful. I give thanks every day and never fail to think of my dear uncle in spirit.

This prayer brings immediate comfort. You feel good the moment you use it, and you feel even better when you see the results you've been hoping for.

No matter what your circumstances, no matter how low you've been, I want you to know that right now *there is real hope.*

I know some will laugh at me, but I don't care. I have all the proof I will ever need. And I keep on getting the proof – every day.

It is the prayer that 'moves mountains', lifts the spirit, and dissolves obstacles.

I know now that my health will always be perfect.

I know now that I will never lack for anything again.

I live in a state of complete reassurance.

This is not to say I am smug. Perish the thought. After what I've been through I am just *so grateful*.

I don't have to worry about my children or anyone else close to me. I use this prayer for them and I just *know* it is answered.

If you need a better memory, better concentration, more confidence, more money, a better job, a promotion, gambling wins – whatever – this prayer will answer your need.

Because it is so simple it does not mean it is not powerful. Probably the reason it has been kept concealed is precisely because it is both simple and potent. I cannot for the life of me see why anything so good should not be available to all.

If you believe, you will be thrilled by the results.

You will then say, like me, that it is the only prayer you will ever need.

15

Your 2018 Birthday Guide

By working with the major astrological influences, you can take control and give your life a better focus. These personal guides show you how to make the most of the positive times and also indicate which days need to be handled with care.

ARIES BORN PEOPLE
Birthdays: 21 March to 20 April inclusive
Planet: Mars. Birthstone: Diamond. Lucky day: Tuesday

Keynote for the Year: *A year when you can slough off the old to make room for the new. Career and family developments may bring you extra demands and responsibilities.*

JANUARY: MAIN TRENDS: 10–11 You are inspired by new horizons and ideas so get out and about as much as you can, freedom is your route to happiness. **18–19** Current trends give a shot in the arm to professional issues; vital information may be made available to you. **20–21** Teamwork and matters conducted in groups will probably be your best area. Expect some positive social developments and perhaps, some unexpected invitations. **KEY DATES: HIGHS 19–20** Planetary energies, especially those that will help you, are strong. **LOWS 3–5; 31** Discipline your thoughts and behaviour so that life's stresses don't lead to frustration.

FEBRUARY: MAIN TRENDS: 10–11 You enjoy being part of a group today and learning from others. **18–19** Another beneficial influence for gatherings with groups of friends. A lively air pervades such situations and you needn't want for company. **20–21** Although trends favour career matters, don't try to run before you can walk and avoid conflict with those in authority. **KEY DATES: HIGHS 19–20** A time for accomplishment in personal plans and schemes. **LOWS 4–5** You may lack enthusiasm, so slow down the pace of life and take stock.

MARCH: MAIN TRENDS: 6–7 You can expect success from innovative schemes today and may be able to influence others positively at work. **17–18** A new romantic interest could be on the horizon so make plans that will involve meeting people. **20–21** Matters of the heart continue to be positively highlighted and all personal contacts benefit from favourable trends. **KEY DATES: HIGHS 18–19** Take your chances and dare to be different, especially in your career. **LOWS 3–5; 31** Prepare for some minor setbacks during this period of low energy.

APRIL: MAIN TRENDS: 1–2 Expect good progress in your objectives now, especially if you've experienced delays of late. **20–21** A splendid time to be in the limelight: romantic, social and leisure pursuits boost your spirits. **24–25** Financial matters should come together as your ability to plan ahead and build upon success strengthens. **KEY DATES: HIGHS 14–15** Trends mean you can talk almost anyone into anything, even superiors at work. **LOWS 1; 27–28** Trends indicate a minor setback at work as your powers of influence wane a little.

MAY: MAIN TRENDS: 13–15 You may get the opportunity to develop some creative and imaginative ideas in your professional life. **19–20** Expect this to be a great day for preparation, especially with business plans. **21–22** You may now reap all the rewards of good teamwork – the more the merrier is the motto. **KEY DATES: HIGHS 12–13** A great time for moving ahead: your powers of influence are at a premium and maintaining a high profile may bring untold benefits. **LOWS 24–26** If day-to-day situations aggravate you, take time out to recharge your batteries.

UNE: MAIN TRENDS: 13–14 Although you are a good communicator and make up for in enthusiasm what you lack in diplomacy, don't assume you have the answers to everything! **21–22** A dynamic phase to throw your vigorous energy into work requiring skill and precision – but don't rush it. **29–30** New encounters may be inspirational as this trend puts you in the social limelight where you attract plenty of good will. **KEY DATES: HIGHS 8–9** Full of optimism, you will not be afraid to use your powers of persuasion. **LOWS 21–22** Think carefully before you make a promise.

ULY: MAIN TRENDS: 1–2 This trend may help clear your mind and leave you ready to tackle problems. New vistas could open up in both personal and professional matters. **10–11** Ambitious and innovative, this is the perfect time to move ahead with dreams and schemes. **22–23** Trends now indicate the need to simplify life and get to the root of problems. A certain personal matter may need a serious rethink. **KEY DATES: HIGHS 5–7** You could feel that there are forces at work helping you to get what you want – which is to the top! **LOWS 18–19** Take a break from ambitious thoughts and don't be too demanding of colleagues.

AUGUST: MAIN TRENDS: 6–7 This influence brings a warmer element to relationships with loved ones. A great period for reliving the good old days. **13–14** A positive influence affects communications and your intellectual ability, enabling you to think and plan in a strategic way. **23–24** Now you are a pioneer, ready to move on and overcome the next challenge. You'll thrive on competition, but may be restless if things stand still. **KEY DATES: HIGHS 1–3; 29–30** Expect to enjoy a little good luck in any enterprising or inventive ideas. **LOWS 14–15** Practical matters may proceed best if you take a subordinate role.

SEPTEMBER: MAIN TRENDS: 6–7 Prioritise your life and put the most focus on what you really value – probably family and loved ones. **9–10** You may get the chance to meet someone new under this influence so keep things varied and interesting. **23–24** Fulfillment may now come from friendships. There may be a happy encounter with an old face from the past. **KEY DATES: HIGHS 25–26** A good time to plan for the future at work, although just about anything you want to do should be rewarding. **LOWS 11–12** Time spent alone right now may be preferable to joining in with others.

OCTOBER: MAIN TRENDS: 10–11 It may be easier than usual to get ahead at work as new information helps put you out in front. **23–24** Prepare for some invaluable help and smooth progress at work as small scale undertakings are met with success. **30–31** Try to vary your routine as much as possible as this is one of those times when you just never know what you might learn. **KEY DATES: HIGHS 22–24** A lucky phase when even errors should be swiftly corrected. **LOWS 8–9** Don't expect everything to go swimmingly – even the best-laid plans can go wrong and some expectations should be played down.

NOVEMBER: MAIN TRENDS: 11–12 Teamwork, especially in social and friendship matters may occupy you much of the time; and in a very useful, informative and pleasant way. **15–16** Organise your time efficiently. Address any issues that arise in the area of joint finance and find practical solutions. **22–23** Focus on the short term where finances are concerned and clear up any outstanding obligations before planning ahead. **KEY DATES: HIGHS 19–20** The planets lend a helping hand to your plans, but your own good judgement comes into play too. **LOWS 4–5** Keep things simple during this emotionally trying period and build your self-confidence.

DECEMBER: MAIN TRENDS: 2–3 Under favourable trends for harmonious communications, a brand new situation may prove stimulating and educational. **12–13** Work hard to keep life on an even keel in the midst of change; measure personal needs against the expectations of others. **21–22** Cheerful and light-hearted, you will want to feel free, travel and pursue intellectual pastimes. **KEY DATES: HIGHS 16–17** With greater freedom for creative self-expression, personal matters should be going especially well. **LOWS 2–3; 29–30** Take care that others don't misconstrue something you have to say.

Angela Merkel

© PA Images

German Chancellor Angela Merkel was born on 17 July 1954 at 6.00 pm in Hamburg. This gives her Sun in sensitive, emotional Cancer; Moon in loyal, humanitarian, socially conscious Aquarius; and a progressive, philosophical Sagittarian ascendant. She's a one-off, as her Sun links with eccentric Uranus, which belies her conventional image. Tough-minded, hard-working Saturn in the 10th (career and profession) plus dynamic Mars in the 1st house (self) makes her driven, energetic and principled. This tenacity of purpose is also what has led her to where she is today.

Proportional representation in Germany means that the government is always formed of a multi-party coalition. As political careers rise and fall and different parties increase in popularity, it seems likely that Angela Merkel has a challenger on her heels for the Chancellorship in the form of relative political newcomer Martin Schulz. As elsewhere in the world, Angela also has to cope with the rise of right-wing populism and also with strong criticism of her 'open-door' refugee policy. Her popularity dented, she has publicly remarked 'If I knew what change in refugee policy the people in Germany want, I would be considering it'. These are unsettling times for Ms Merkel and, interestingly, the planetary picture for the German people over the next year is rather inward looking. Although the astrological indications for Merkel's victory are quite good – even if only by a narrow margin – Old Moore also sees a tendency for the German people to look for a politician who they feel will put them first, and if this mood prevails, this could tip the balance to Schulz.

So – Chancellor or not – what's next for Angela Merkel? Towards the end of 2017, lucky Jupiter contacts her chart, making this a good time professionally. This could indicate good relations in the coalition and some popular announcements to enhance her poll ratings. However, her continued stance towards immigration might cause some damage to her rising appeal for voters as she's not about to give up what she values for popularity's sake. Her chart also suggests that personal and domestic concerns may make heavy demands on her time in 2018, leading her to revisit the past and her roots and turn *away* from the outside world. She may start to feel that politics has become more trouble than it's worth. These pressures may build to a crisis in April and May as Pluto makes her question her own values. Any time up until the influence of Uranus is restored in July and August we could hear news of a shock resignation as Angela looks for the freedom to explore other avenues. In some area, professional or personal, it seems that the second half of 2018 could mark an ending and a new beginning.

TAURUS BORN PEOPLE

Birthdays: 21 April to 21 May inclusive
Planet: Venus. Birthstone: Emerald. Lucky day: Friday

Keynote for the Year: You should see growth and rewards in personal relationships, whether new or old. A good time to join forces with others – this can prove lucky!

JANUARY: MAIN TRENDS: 12–13 The pace of life picks up and you can make use of new information coming your way and talk others around to your viewpoint. **18–19** This is perhaps not the easiest influence for relationships; insist on some privacy and solitude if you need it. **20–21** You can benefit by cultivating contacts with influential people. Listen to others and don't be in a rush to do everything your own way. **KEY DATES: HIGHS 25–26** As your luck increases you may enjoy the feeling that all is right with the world. **LOWS 10–11** Unforeseen results may lead to impatience. Keep calm and take things easily.

FEBRUARY: MAIN TRENDS: 10–11 Life proceeds at a fairly brisk pace. Talks with others should prove pleasant and inspiring. **18–19** Let go of thoughts that have preoccupied you recently, adopt a new attitude and move onwards and upwards. **23–24** Doing your own thing is the key to happiness right now, particularly in your love life. You simply need to be yourself. **KEY DATES: HIGHS 21–22** Get major plans underway as the tide of favour now goes your way. You should find that your expectations are fulfilled. **LOWS 6–8** Try not to focus on obstacles in your way or do things the hard way but take things easier for a day or so.

MARCH: MAIN TRENDS: 8–9 Your ego is over-inflated right now, but you can get away with most things as your personality shines brightly. **17–18** A positive influence under which relationships should run harmoniously. There should be time for some romance, too. **20–21** You should enjoy the best of both worlds (business and pleasure) now as you seek to develop material and financial plans. **KEY DATES: HIGHS 20–21** A good period for making fresh starts and taking a little measured gamble. **LOWS 6–7** Even if you are stuck with the day-to-day routines don't make *everything* a grind and take time out for some fun when you can.

APRIL: MAIN TRENDS: 16–17 Your social life and friendships are wonderfully enhanced with Venus now in your sign. You're great at bringing people together with a positive attitude. **20–21** A lucrative influence when it comes to the practical and financial world; joint money matters are your particular forte. **24–25** A peak for vitality when you will enjoy pushing ahead with any kind of plan or just soaking up the social limelight. **KEY DATES: HIGHS 16–18** A cautious risk taken in either your personal or your professional life could have a lucky outcome. **LOWS 2–3; 29–30** Obligations may test your patience today and, with limited energy, pressure could get to you. Take a step back for some breathing space if you need to.

MAY: MAIN TRENDS: 12–13 Gather information wherever you can as what you learn could change things. **19–20** Take a broad approach to life: try out all sorts of different interests, intellectual and cultural. **21–22** Joint finances may receive a boost. Generally a lucky phase when you will benefit by moving on from anything you have outgrown. **KEY DATES: HIGHS 14–15** Get an early start with all important projects and be open to communications that could benefit you. **LOWS 27–28** Be aware that taking action without due caution could make your plans go wrong.

JUNE: MAIN TRENDS: 13–14 Your lively and sparkling personality comes to the fore and you are interesting company. **21–22** A good time to focus on financial matters – some positive thinking will almost certainly work wonders. **29–30** A helpful influence work wise that should enable you to get matters into good order; don't miss any opportunities. **KEY DATES: HIGHS 10–11** A fortunate period when you can very easily persuade others on to your side – make the most of it! **LOWS 23–24** Enjoy a time of peace and quiet domestically and avoid any temptation to make waves.

JULY: MAIN TRENDS: 1–2 You enjoy the company of others in groups or associations. Business enterprises also make progress due to good teamwork. **10–11** Your insight may help you solve problems as right now you better understand people's motivations, their strengths and weaknesses. **22–23** Withdraw from the social mainstream to satisfy your inner or spiritual concerns and opt for a simple lifestyle. **KEY DATES: HIGHS 8–9** A good time to initiate new projects, as you are so full of good ideas. **LOWS 20–21** Prepare for one or two obstacles or temporary setbacks at work but bear in mind that this is just a passing phase.

AUGUST: MAIN TRENDS: 6–7 Enjoy a pleasurable social period when you are at your most popular. **13–14** Trends suggest you will enjoy some solitude and perhaps embark upon a journey of self-discovery. **23–24** Don't allow your ego and enthusiasm to lead you to promise more than you can deliver. **KEY DATES: HIGHS 4–5; 31** A little help from influential people may help you to lighten your responsibilities. **LOWS 16–18** Don't be afraid to hang back a little professionally in order to deal with certain personal matters. Focus on simpler tasks to reserve your energy.

SEPTEMBER: MAIN TRENDS: 6–7 Take care over financial decisions as they could mark the key moment in your progress. **9–10** Trends suggest you could receive some help with something practical, but also that you may be pre-occupied with a health issue. **23–24** The planets give a lift to matters of leisure and pleasure so get out and enjoy yourself now. **KEY DATES: HIGHS 1; 27–29** Under some lucky trends, you may get the chance to make strides with a recent pet project. **LOWS 13–14** Keep to the tried-and-tested path and avoid risks of any sort at this time.

OCTOBER: MAIN TRENDS: 12–13 Trends indicate some developments at work, although you will have put in a lot of effort to achieve them. **23–24** Emotional issues could leave you feeling defeated. Don't be too hard on yourself if not everything works out as you feel it should. **30–31** Certain goals you have striven for may prove to bring little satisfaction. This may be the time for an overhaul of your plans and objectives. **KEY DATES: HIGHS 25–26** You are strong both mentally and physically – and optimistic too. **LOWS 10–11** Disagreements over everyday matters and gossip can leave you feeling unfulfilled. Don't bottle up important convictions.

NOVEMBER: MAIN TRENDS: 11–12 Don't make instant professional decisions on a whim right now, but equally don't ignore any important developments that may arise. **15–16** A good day to take a trip or plan something exciting and new with a friend or colleague. **23–24** The recent swift pace of life may slacken, giving you more time for personal indulgences. Family and domestic life are your real priorities now. **KEY DATES: HIGHS 21–22** Trends help you to find the right path so where important objectives are concerned, don't be afraid to take a few calculated chances. **LOWS 7–8** Your efficiency at work and your ability to focus could suffer just at the moment, so avoid making plans that could later go awry and concentrate on routine tasks instead.

DECEMBER: MAIN TRENDS: 2–3 Follow your heart when it comes to seeking new intellectual pastures: there is much to be said for travel, culture and a freewheeling attitude to life. **12–13** Avoid any tendency to take loved ones for granted or demand too much of your own way; this attitude could prove self-defeating. **21–22** You are happy and comfortable at home and the resultant sense of security does you the world of good. **KEY DATES: HIGHS 18–20** A great time to bring others around to your way of thinking as Lady Luck lends you a helping hand! **LOWS 4–5; 31** If it's a challenge to keep on top of things work wise, take things one at a time.

Brexit – What the Planets Tell Us

On 23 June 2017 voters across the UK cast their votes in a referendum to decide whether the United Kingdom should stay in the European Union or leave. At 10.00 pm that evening the polls closed and the decision had been made. It was at that point, 10.00 pm on 23 June that the die was cast and the process began. Old Moore therefore looks primarily at the astrological chart set for that momentous point in our history to see how we can expect the negotiations to exit the European Union to proceed.

THE BREXIT CHART

With Capricorn rising and the Sun in the watery sign of Cancer there is no doubt that the negotiations will be a long hard slog. The Sun was in opposition to Saturn, Lord of time, so we cannot expect any sudden breakthroughs and with the Moon also involved in this opposition the whole business is likely to be attended by a highly-charged emotional atmosphere, with accusations of posturing on both sides. Mars was opposed to the Ascendant, meaning that we can expect significant recriminations by all parties, at least during the first part of the negotiations.

One positive in the Brexit chart was that it took place at the time of a potent New Moon, hardly a better moment for clearing the decks and striking out for something new and different. From this perspective at least, no better day could have been chosen and, while we cannot expect an easy path ahead, there is also support from Mercury, king of communication and sweet Venus, in her own sign of Taurus.

THE SINGLE MARKET

Many UK voters would wish to retain the benefits accruing from membership of the EU Single Market but politically this appears an unlikely prospect. Astrologically, the crowding of planets in the sign of Cancer may indicate a better ultimate outcome in this regard than might first seem the case. There are a number of transits, especially related to Jupiter, which suggest that a clearer view of Britain's trading position post-Brexit will be evident by the middle of December 2017. In many ways the Brexit chart begins to open out like a flower after the start of 2018. This is most likely to indicate new trade deals with economies outside the EU. Old Moore suggests that, all things considered, the UK's negotiators will not be successful in achieving everything they would wish in this direction but conciliatory Cancer could ensure a 'special deal' dreamed up by a European Union that, even despite itself, has a vested interest in a successful outcome. The chart does reveal that there is some duplicity to be expected, plus the possibility of a restructuring of the whole EU in the spring and summer of 2018. Negotiators will need patience and, with Mercury in Cancer conjunct Sun and Moon, to strive for uncompromising honesty.

IMMIGRATION

This aspect of the negotiations appears to be highlighted positively in the Brexit chart. This may seem the most contentious of issues as talks begin to heat up and a Capricorn ascendant to Mars opposition once again indicates backbiting, recriminations and false accusations until the spring of 2018. Old Moore feels that any deadlock may be broken by the UK, under the fortunate transits of Jupiter in March and April of 2018, leading to the announcement of a unilateral decision regarding immigrant workers from the EU. The prediction is for an outcome post-Brexit which may be described by politicians as different from before but which is essentially almost identical. The strength of watery Cancer in the Brexit chart also indicates an increase rather than a decrease of immigrant workers from parts of the world far from Europe.

THE UK'S DEBT TO THE EU

Early indications are that this will be the most contentious and hard-fought part of the Brexit negotiations but while there are a number of oppositions in the Brexit chart there are few squares and a wealth of good aspects, particularly relating to Venus. Negotiators on both sides of the Channel should focus on what the UK shares with Europe. Jupiter is in conciliatory Libra and it is possible that common adversity, most likely related to terrorism, will bring politicians closer together by the early summer of 2018, increasing the spirit of compromise which will have to be made on both sides. A new and possibly neutral character emerging in the negotiating team around May 2018 might help both sides to come to a mutually agreeable conclusion.

IN CONCLUSION

The reality of Brexit has led to bruised egos, particularly for our European cousins, and also to a sense of dislocation and even disbelief in our own islands. The UK has been for some time in a volatile astrological position and Brexit forms only one part of these long-lasting trends. Despite the doubt and uncertainty that prevails as Old Moore writes these words, the shoots of a new harvest are already beginning to grow. The Brexit chart shows that we must walk forward with confidence – in ourselves, in our European allies and in the decision that has been made democratically – no matter how difficult that might be. The Brexit chart indicates that we must leave negativity behind us, judge matters wisely and honestly, and maintain the sense of fair play for which the British people are known across Europe. Two years on from the date of the fateful decision, the United Kingdom will still be part of the European continent but will also be playing on a world stage. It is Old Moore's opinion that it may not be until that time that some people face the fact that the British people were never ideally suited to the European Union.

GEMINI BORN PEOPLE
Birthdays: 22 May to 21 June inclusive
Planet: Mercury. Birthstone: Agate. Lucky day: Wednesday

Keynote for the Year: *Make the most of opportunities at work this year. Emotional relationships and joint finance may bring new responsibilities.*

JANUARY: MAIN TRENDS: 10–11 New intellectual interests may hold a lot of appeal for you now. Try to include others in them when you can. **18–19** Explore the wide blue yonder – the more you get out and see what life outdoors has to offer, the better. **20–21** This is the best time for a 'clear out' in your life, when you should dispense with any deadwood that's been holding you back. **KEY DATES: HIGHS 27–28** New ideas you have up your sleeve may now see the light of day as you feel inclined to push your luck a little. **LOWS 12–14** You could experience some frustrations so take things easily for a day or so.

FEBRUARY: MAIN TRENDS: 11–12 You have a need to express yourself creatively in one form or another and the confidence to take large strides. **18–19** Today you communicate easily with others and are interested in what they think – perhaps because there is new information you can glean. **20–21** This trend is likely to bring out the best in you as you get on with different people on an equal footing. Be willing to put others first. **KEY DATES: HIGHS 23–24** The bigger and more far-reaching your aims are, the better at this time. Go for it! **LOWS 9–10** Don't waste time on futile endeavours that are just not working, instead cut your losses.

MARCH: MAIN TRENDS: 6–7 Trends bring practical issues into focus, especially those connected with money. It's now time to consolidate and build upon them. **17–18** A great time to be on the move, especially if you use your communication skills to your advantage. **20–21** Relationships benefit from some good trends and you shouldn't have to try too hard to win over others or find yourself in good company. **KEY DATES: HIGHS 22–23** Make the most of the fortunate influences that surround you at this time. **LOWS 8–9** You could encounter some stumbling blocks in your personal progress so only proceed with what you know will work.

APRIL: MAIN TRENDS: 1–2 A good period for travel and mental recreation, though you may well spend so much time in search of fresh pastures that little else gets done. **21–22** You thrive on challenges, especially new ones at work, and hone your skills as a result. **24–25** Time to 'declutter': decide what can easily be jettisoned from your life, simplify and move on. **KEY DATES: HIGHS 19–20** Good trends pave the way towards professional success. Time to roll the dice and see what Lady Luck has in store. **LOWS 4–5** A phase when you may be temporarily drained of physical vitality and need frequent periods of rest to regain your strength.

MAY: MAIN TRENDS: 13–14 Your achievements peak in professional matters and you should find it easy to get your own way. **19–20** All types of partnerships take on greater significance now as you attract people who are interesting and inspirational. **21–22** With boundless energy and vitality you should accomplish a lot towards your personal goals. **KEY DATES: HIGHS 16–17** Your own effort is all you should need to influence things to good effect. **LOWS 2–3; 29–30** Not a time when you can expect a great deal of progress or satisfaction, so keep your expectations simple.

JUNE: MAIN TRENDS: 14–15 The domestic scene holds a new appeal for you; a good time to talk with parents and family. **21–22** You may find certain decisions have an element of trial and error about them and moves made today may prove far from decisive. **29–30** Be rid of anything unnecessary, separate the wheat from chaff and concentrate on important things. **KEY DATES: HIGHS 12–13** You

Vladimir Putin

© PA Images

Of one thing there is no doubt: Vladimir Putin is an immensely important global figure. To some he has successfully weathered the recent economic storm, resisted Western influence and 'made Russia great again'. To others, his involvement with neighbouring countries and the Middle East, his repressive social policies at home and, more recently, allegations of his tampering – via computer hacking – in the US Presidential election make him someone to be extremely wary of. Whatever your view of Putin's Russia, let's take a look at the coming astrological influences to see if the planets indicate a return to power after the elections in March 2018.

Vladimir Putin was born in Leningrad on 7 October 1952 at 9.30 am which gives him Sun in Libra, part of a conjunction with Saturn and Neptune in his twelfth house, the house of shadowy, secret goings on – very apt for a former member of the KGB! Planets in the twelfth house often don't express themselves positively, but here hard-headed Saturn is conjunct Mercury, the planet of thinking and communication, which suggests a logical, steely, quick-thinking mind, as does subtle, passionate (even vengeful) Scorpio rising. We must also factor in power-driven Pluto on the MC (public image/career) making him well acquainted with danger and high-level conflicts and giving him an instinctive understanding of power. This tough and resilient side to his character, together with his good organisational skills, has helped him stand up to his enemies and detractors with some considerable force and skill.

Massive political challenges are indicated on Mr Putin's chart in late 2017 when the pressure from Pluto and Saturn will test his mettle as leader. He may now find confrontation from all sides over an international crisis. It's just as well that he now starts a personal cycle of potential opportunity, as progressive Jupiter crosses his ascendant (the self/personality). When we get into 2018, the planetary picture indicates that Vladimir Putin will remain high in opinion polls, and as the Russian elections roll around he'll be in a positively bullish mood. There are two astrological suggestions in March that he'll carry on as President – the Venus/Mars factor, indicating continued affection from the Russian population, and the 'progressed' Moon–Sun effect, indicating a 'homecoming', a sense that he's being returned to his 'rightful' place. As for relations with the West, there is no particular pointer to hostilities on the Russian national chart in 2018; if anything it suggests improving relations with both Europe and the US. During the summer, barring an indication of health problems in August, things could improve for Putin as more economic sanctions may be lifted from his shoulders if this has not, in fact, already happened.

may be able to persuade an influential figure to help you with a current ambition. **LOWS 26–27** A general lull when little of significance happens for you in your competitive and ambitious endeavours.

JULY: MAIN TRENDS: 1–2 Fulfillment comes through travel and you are likely to enjoy the company of people you meet. **12–13** Communicative and responsive to others, you enjoy your social life even if decisiveness is not your main talent. **25–26** Capitalise on the current planetary trends, which bring out the best in you and firm up securities. **KEY DATES: HIGHS 10–11** Lady Luck may put you in the right place at the right time now. **LOWS 22–24** Take heed of your instinct to forego the limelight and enjoy some rest and recuperation.

AUGUST: MAIN TRENDS: 8–9 The desire for fresh fields is stronger than ever, and seeking out change and variety could lead to some intriguing results. **13–14** Your love life runs smoothly and amicably and you can look forward to friendly responses. **23–24** Short trips and time spent with others might be productive and the chance to communicate new ideas may present itself. **KEY DATES: HIGHS 6–7** Don't be afraid to ask for something you need as you speed towards your desired objectives. **LOWS 19–20** Career commitments may leave less time for leisure, but effective planning will enable you to live up to your responsibilities.

SEPTEMBER: MAIN TRENDS: 6–7 If you are frustrated by the feeling that you are being held back, take a look at a plan and see if it requires second thoughts. **9–10** Trends suggest you'll love to try new things and experiment at this time – follow your curiosity as it could lead to brand new interests. **23–24** A good time to develop your personal resourcefulness as the planets enable you to dispense with old attachments and make new plans. **KEY DATES: HIGHS 2–4; 30** You find the confidence to try new things that are audacious and unusual now. **LOWS 15–16** Prepare to have to contend with some limitations either in ambitions or personal relationships.

OCTOBER: MAIN TRENDS: 10–11 A warm phase when you can bring out the best in others; look for the best in everyone. **23–24** An excellent time for hogging the limelight, you can expect to be the centre of attention or to make some lucky strides in a personal matter. **30–31** The green light is on where progress is to be made so you should think big. Some ingenious thinking may save the day. **KEY DATES: HIGHS 1; 27–28** You will want to be busy in some way as the beneficial high continues apace; you are capable in all areas of your life and your charisma is strong. **LOWS 12–14** You enter a planetary lull so the wisest course of action is to keep life simple and undemanding.

NOVEMBER: MAIN TRENDS: 11–12 Consolidate and organise your affairs in a material sense. Financial developments look especially promising right now. **15–16** A new alliance or relationship may bring out the best in you and allow you to be yourself. Leisure and pleasure is favourably highlighted. **21–22** Now in a fairly progressive phase, trends suggest that you should order your schedule at work so that it does not dominate every area of your life. **KEY DATES: HIGHS 23–24** Personal choices made today may be considered fortunate in the long run. **LOWS 9–10** Suspend any major decision-making and enjoy a little self-indulgence by way of compensation.

DECEMBER: MAIN TRENDS: 2–3 Enjoy time at home as domestic relationships should be rewarding and fulfilling. **12–13** Matters in the practical world may be on the up and up. A good time to exchange views at work and enlist someone's co-operation. **23–24** You have the ability to handle important business and move ahead more swiftly than ever – this is where your strengths lie now. **KEY DATES: HIGHS 21–22** Trends indicate that good luck is flowing towards you and this is all that's needed to make the day go with a swing. **LOWS 6–7** If you are lacking in the practical ability required for certain tasks, put them aside for another day.

John Bishop

© PA Images

Comedian, TV presenter and interviewer John Bishop's star has been on the rise for a number of years. Critics have called him 'Britain's top comic' and his appearance on Forbes' list of Highest Paid Comedians underscores his growing success. John's fans would say he has earned every bit of the acclaim he enjoys. But what are the astrological keys to his character and his success?

John Joseph Bishop was born on 30 November 1966, giving him the Sun and seductive Venus in Sagittarius. At once this makes him instantly appealing and attractive to others – he certainly knows how to stir people's affections. In addition, the Sun makes a helpful contact with his ruling planet, big-hearted Jupiter. This means he puts out lots of generosity and trust into the world and then gets it back tenfold. His Moon is in sensitive Cancer, reinforcing his love of the past, of home, family and roots – for him, home is where the heart is. He's certainly a proud Liverpudlian and, indeed, a fanatical supporter of Liverpool FC. Sagittarius is often associated with sporting prowess so it comes as no surprise that John's first choice of career was as a footballer, playing for non-league teams Hyde and Southport.

Mercury conjoined empathic Neptune means that John has the ability to not only empathise with the opinions of others but also with their hardships and suffering. Perhaps this is why he's almost as famous for his charity work as he is for comedy, raising a massive £4.2m for Sport Relief in 2012. Perhaps this understanding side to John's personality is also why he's a committed vegetarian. In 2013, animal charity PETA declared him to be one of the 'sexiest vegetarians' of that year! But John Bishop is much more than this: feisty Mars linked with powerful Pluto–Uranus makes a harsh contact with gritty Saturn. This is his hard, resilient, determined side and this means that if he discovers obstacles he'll surely find a way to overcome them. When required, there is iron in his soul.

2018 looks like being an excellent year for John. In March and October the Neptune effect means he'll want to give something back to the world. He'll almost certainly be involved in high-profile charity events around now. In the summer, especially June and July, Pluto's influence takes over making this a good time for a spring clean, not just of the home but also in terms of a review of his life to look for any beneficial changes. This Pluto influence makes it possible to abandon anything that isn't worthwhile or working out successfully. The real boon, however, comes in November, when lucky Jupiter moves into John's Sun sign heralding the start of a twelve-month period of new potential for growth and valuable exciting opportunities.

Personal Signs in Chinese Astrology

In Chinese astrology, your character type is defined by the year of your birth. Each year is associated with one of 12 animals. The cycle of animals repeats in the sequence listed below, beginning with the rat. Years of the rat are 1948, 1960, 1972 and so on. The Ox is therefore 1949, 1961 and so on, or you can search online for your sign. For January/February birthdays, check online when Chinese new year fell in your year – if it was after your birthday, your sign will be the one of the year before.

RAT: Clever and resourceful, the rat is the charmer, intelligent, practical and quick-witted. Social types, they make loyal friends, but can be opinionated and a little cunning at times.

OX: Reserved, practical and inflexible. Meticulous planners, they don't put up with nonsense and can be stubborn, although they can be relied on for practical skills, common sense and strength of purpose.

TIGER: Unpredictable and with a fierce love of freedom, the tiger has a natural magnetism and strong independent streak. Creative and tireless, tigers are apt to change their minds.

RABBIT: Don't be fooled by the mild-mannered and home-loving rabbit, there's a manipulative streak and a desire to succeed which can push you out of the way if they can't diplomatically bring you round to their point of view. A great sensualist, but not always good under pressure.

DRAGON: The dragon represents a positive, life-enhancing strength, sometimes impulsive, always energetic and assertive. Perhaps not the most patient person you'll ever meet, if there's a negative side, it's their tendency to be self-opinionated and an inability to apologise!

SNAKE: Snakes are essentially reserved creatures. Elegant, charming, kind and sensual, they make loyal friends, but there's a part that very few get to know. Highly astute, it's hard to get the better of them, nor a good idea to make enemies of them, as they could strike when you least expect it.

HORSE: An exuberant nature and quick brain characterise this natural actor and perfect salesperson. Always interesting, with an eccentric and ingenious streak, they have a great sense of fun, although they don't always know what they are talking about and can be cantankerous if crossed.

GOAT: Refined, soft-hearted and intellectual, these people tend to be sensual and sometimes extravagant, although they can be insecure and use a natural reserve to protect them from what they see as a threatening world. Don't upset them, as they have a long memory.

MONKEY: Always active, sexy and versatile, these can be the know-it-alls if they get all their own way, but criticism can wound their over-size ego. They relish a challenge, and are more than capable of sorting out most problems quickly and efficiently.

ROOSTER: Sometimes fussy and fastidious, but with an amazing capacity for accuracy, these people speak their minds, have unbounded curiosity, and are reliable and trustworthy. Very tidy-minded, they won't put up with other people's mess – literal or otherwise.

DOG: Communicative and excitable, this is a mercurial character, usually optimistic but inclined to be negative if things start to go wrong. Charming, hard-working and affectionate, they are likeable characters who make good friends, but are best not cornered.

PIG: Hard-working and shy, these sensual people respond well to attention. Although it is not easy to understand them, they make true friends. Stubborn, once committed, they rarely lose a battle.

THE ELEMENTS: Each year is associated with an element as well as with an animal, which further defines your characteristics. The elements change every two years, so 1952 and 1953 are water years, 1954 and 1955 are wood years, and so on. You can find the element for your year on-line. Water people are creative, compassionate, kind and understanding. Wood people are warm, considerate, generous and co-operative. Fire people are dynamic, purposeful and strong. Earth people are patient, hard-working, reliable and sometimes stubborn. Metal people have strength of character and determination.

2018 – Year of the Dog

Chinese astrology works on a slightly different time scale from the more familiar Western branch of the study, and because of this Chinese New Year does not commence in 2018 until 16 February. Until that time, the world remains under the rulership of the Rooster, the influence of which has been felt throughout society for the last twelve months or so. The ancient Chinese scribes identified this period as being one of deep talking, with pauses for consideration regarding what has gone before and what lies ahead. International negotiations during these few weeks may run successfully and amicably.

However, from 16 February the influence changes somewhat as the year of the Dog dawns. Often thought of as being similar to the Western zodiac sign of Libra, Dog years are times when we look at our values more closely than we might in other years. During Dog years, there are strong diplomatic tendencies and a need to put right difficulties from the past before moving on steadily. The Dog is generally peaceful, which sometimes means that there is less violence in the world and making the year a time during which the forces of law and order predominate. Hasty actions are definitely not recommended while the Dog is in charge and this trend extends even to countries that have not seen eye-to-eye in the past – their leaders may take time out to reflect and reappraise. Religious and nationalistic tendencies should also be less pronounced under this influence.

The element associated with the Dog in 2018 is Earth. This pairing adds to the steady and reliable qualities of the ever-affable Dog, and if we carry this through to look at the global significance, this should lead to a period of greater stability with leaders more willing to talk to each other than has been the case for a few years past. Where there has been doubt or confusion things are likely to look more settled; whatever the Chinese sign, it is a fact that people generally tend to relax more under the influence of the Earth element. All in all, the Dog and Earth are a positive – if somewhat quiet – combination.

If you were born under the year of the Dog, roughly after the end of January in the years 1922, 1934, 1946, 1958, 1970, 1982, 1994 or 2006, like your counterpart in the animal world, forever known as 'man's best friend', you are likely to possess the best possible traits of human nature. You have a good sense of loyalty and fidelity and tend to be very honest in your dealings with both those close to you and the world at large, although it isn't difficult for you to keep secrets when you feel it necessary. Of course there are times when you can be stubborn and it is true that some people might consider you to be strange or eccentric. You won't mind this if you are secure in your sense of self-worth, as you should be. You revel in good company and tend to be very loyal to your loved ones, relatives and friends. Reflect upon these excellent qualities at the start of this, your own Chinese year, and enjoy all the promise that it holds in store for you.

CANCER BORN PEOPLE
Birthdays: 22 June to 22 July inclusive
Planet: Moon. Birthstone: Ruby. Lucky day: Monday

Keynote for the Year: *Love life and leisure are where all your chances for growth and fulfillment lie this year. Creative activities are also an area through which you can develop.*

JANUARY: MAIN TRENDS: 11–12 With good ideas for improving work methods with co-workers, you may now be able to get to the root of problems. **18–19** Continuing favourable trends professionally mean that there may be more than one way of succeeding now, so think outside the box! **20–21** The pace of life picks up merrily and you can make use of new input and information. **KEY DATES: HIGHS 1–2; 29–30** Take the initiative when it comes to change and renewal in any arena. **LOWS 15–16** Stumbling blocks in the pace of your progress may mean that plans fail to get off the ground. Take some rest instead.

FEBRUARY: MAIN TRENDS: 14–15 Utilise your confidence to try new things in pursuit of your goals. **18–19** Trends make you naturally outgoing and help you to make friends easily, so it should not be difficult to enlist the help of others with group projects. **20–21** You may have the opportunity to improve your current financial status and a fresh initiative may take you in a new direction, but avoid any unnecessary risks. **KEY DATES: HIGHS 25–26** Professionally speaking, you seem to be ready for just about any challenge. **LOWS 11–13** A quiet phase, not really the best time to go boldly forth. Keep a lid on certain ambitions for now.

MARCH: MAIN TRENDS: 6–7 Events today will remind you of how much significant information you have at your disposal that could help you get ahead. **17–18** Take advantage of a nice trend by being with friends as people are well disposed to you. **20–21** You thrive in the social mainstream and especially enjoy exchanging views with others, although you enjoy learning just for its own sake right now. **KEY DATES: HIGHS 24–25** Express your individuality and follow your competitive instincts – it would seem that success will follow. **LOWS 10–13** Avoid the potential pitfalls inherent in certain situations that are no longer working effectively.

APRIL: MAIN TRENDS: 1–2 Your love life should be working out well now, giving you lots of confidence and making this a happy period. **20–21** A marvellous influence for domestic matters, particularly nostalgic ones – why not have an old friend over and reminisce? **24–25** Rely on your intuition when it comes to problem solving as you now excel at analysing and sorting out practical details of any kind. **KEY DATES: HIGHS 21–22** Focus all your energy on making strides professionally or personally during this high-powered phase. **LOWS 7–8** If you are called upon to resolve a mini crisis, it might prove beneficial to let partners have the last word.

MAY: MAIN TRENDS: 13–15 Romantically there may be big things happening now; a situation may need an important decision with regard to your true feelings. **19–20** There's a desire to get things done as quickly as possible. Don't go overboard on spending sprees as your finances may fluctuate somewhat. **21–22** In a sensitive mood today, your feelings can be easily hurt. You may choose to spend time alone for this reason. **KEY DATES: HIGHS 18–19** A busy spell when your energy and ambition drives you, and rewarding in many ways. **LOWS 4–5; 31** From an astrological point of view it's time to slow down and rest – this might come as a welcome relief.

JUNE: MAIN TRENDS: 13–14 With confidence and an attitude geared towards success, you can get ahead nicely by taking the initiative. **21–22** Rid yourself of certain plans and ideas that are not working and keep life as simple as possible. You should not be lacking in emotional support. **26–27** Now the pace at work may slacken and personal matters assume greater significance. A good time for imaginative and creative pursuits. **KEY DATES: HIGHS 14–15** A positive mental attitude plus swift action – the surprise attack – brings benefits now. **LOWS 1–2; 28–29** Not really the most favourable trend for making major decisions – you may have to deal with tricky situations.

JULY: MAIN TRENDS: 1–2 While business partnerships may work better than ever now, in love you may need to remain firm on a particular matter. **10–11** The company of loved ones and partners brings you rewards today. There may be invitations to exciting social gatherings. **22–23** A period of high ego when you may insist on having things all your own way. You should enjoy your time in the limelight! **KEY DATES: HIGHS 12–13** As lucky trends surround you, this is the day to start new projects and push ahead as much as possible. **LOWS 25–26** Ambitions should not be your priority – instead spend time enjoying rest and recuperation.

AUGUST: MAIN TRENDS: 6–7 Put your good ideas to use, make swift decisions and show others your versatility. **13–14** Your emotions may be running high, especially if, as trends indicate, you have to make some kind of break with the past. **24–25** A nostalgic phase when you get the most fulfillment from your family; a great time to entertain at home. **KEY DATES: HIGHS 8–9** A potentially lucky phase during which you may make important changes as you take steps towards future goals. **LOWS 21–23** A temporary lull when your spirits may be rather flat – don't expect too much of yourself.

SEPTEMBER: MAIN TRENDS: 6–7 Your chart indicates a little luck for you now, so focus on material consolidation to further improve your position. **9–10** As trends move on, you may now be lacking in practical discipline financially. Beware of an unrealistic attitude to money. **23–24** Your personal magnetism is one of your main strengths making this a great time for using the gift of the gab. **KEY DATES: HIGHS 5–6** The success you can achieve – both in your professional and personal life – is now huge. Go for your goals! **LOWS 17–19** A troubling sense of doubt may accompany your decisions now so put major plans on ice for a couple of days.

OCTOBER: MAIN TRENDS: 10–11 Work and responsibility may feel burdensome now, so delegate minor obligations to others if you can. **23–24** A high spot for your social life when you should enjoy great popularity and thrive in the limelight. **27–28** You enjoy change, variety, and making new contacts – and it could be that you have one or two new and interesting avenues to explore. **KEY DATES: HIGHS 2–3; 29–30** Motivation is the key to success, and this trend helps the tide of fortune flow your way. **LOWS 15–16** During the monthly low, as usual you can expect one or two hitches; you may also have trouble keeping appointments.

NOVEMBER: MAIN TRENDS: 9–10 Money is top of your agenda today – a great period to do business, or even for a little cautious flutter! **15–16** Socially you should be in good cheer; and you may want to be on the move – travel can really broaden the mind. **22–23** It may now be difficult to work under the leadership of others as you prefer to be a leader and want things done yesterday. **KEY DATES: HIGHS 25–26** The way ahead lies in innovation and change and certain lucky influences assist you down these paths. **LOWS 11–13** A minor lull when you may find yourself temporarily less than enthusiastic.

DECEMBER: MAIN TRENDS: 2–3 It should be smooth sailing at work as you benefit from talks and negotiations with those in authority. **12–13** A personal relationship may prove very supportive of certain long-range plans and you may find others' input invaluable. **21–22** Again, relationships are working well; a new friendship may develop, one that will be valuable in future days. **KEY DATES: HIGHS 23–24** You can channel enormous enthusiasm about the future into your long term plans – which means you can virtually move mountains! **LOWS 9–10** Don't try to forge ahead as usual but take some time out.

LEO BORN PEOPLE
Birthdays: 23 July to 23 August inclusive
Planet: Sun. Birthstone: Sapphire. Lucky day: Sunday

Keynote for the Year: *In the workplace there may be many a lesson to be learned this year, but all the comforts of home and family are your main priority in 2018.*

JANUARY: MAIN TRENDS: 11–12 You have no shortage of good ideas and can successfully handle several different tasks at the same time, bringing a big boost to your social life. **15–16** Time to rid yourself of outworn situations, but you may have to be quite ruthless in saying goodbye. **20–21** Your ability to take the starring role socially should be put to some practical use today, especially around those who have the potential to assist your plans. **KEY DATES: HIGHS 3–4; 31** Favourable trends may help you reap the rewards of recent professional efforts. **LOWS 17–19** Under this planetary lull even careful planning may run adrift so take some time out.

FEBRUARY: MAIN TRENDS: 6–7 A positive social influence that should bring out the best in you. You bring out the best in others, too, especially while working as a team. **17–18** Finances may tend to fluctuate now and you may have to focus on remaining steady in the midst of change – whether you like it or not. **20–21** Don't be afraid to branch into new areas as they may bring gains intellectually and culturally. **KEY DATES: HIGHS 27–28** The planets bring you a boon and some good luck along with it. Test your luck a little, but always avoid undue risk. **LOWS 14–15** If you suffer one or two setbacks try not to blame others for the disappointment.

MARCH: MAIN TRENDS: 6–7 Trends bring a boost to your ambitions at work, helping you to focus on plans for the future and make something solid of them. **17–18** An enjoyable, carefree period, good for social outings and day trips, perhaps with your intimate circle. **20–21** You may need to decide whether you want to continue with something as it is or institute changes of one kind or another – the time may be ripe for something new. **KEY DATES: HIGHS 26–28** Put your luck to the test during this green-light period when everything seems to go your way. **LOWS 13–14** Maintain a low profile and wind down certain plans for a day or so.

APRIL: MAIN TRENDS: 1–2 Trends make you attractive to others; a good time for co-operation and interaction on new projects. **20–21** You will enjoy the kind of company you are keeping now, especially if it's connected with your past. **26–27** A favourable period for advancing with short-term plans and career ambitions; at work push your luck a little with those in a position of influence. **KEY DATES: HIGHS 23–24** Another good time to take a little chance, you may be surprised at how willing others are to help. **LOWS 9–11** If you seem to be carrying a heavy burden, narrow down your options and choose goals that are more realistic.

MAY: MAIN TRENDS: 13–15 Social meetings with new people are likely and someone in particular might make you feel good with their attention. **19–20** A good period to communicate with others, especially about new ideas. Aim for diversity and variety as these are the keys to satisfaction. **22–23** Don't allow minor issues to overwhelm you but instead take a step back and reflect on your progress so far. **KEY DATES: HIGHS 20–21** It's important to you to get your message across to others, so much so that others notice how communicative you are. **LOWS 7–8** If you push ahead with your ambitions now, expect to have to compromise at some point.

JUNE: MAIN TRENDS: 13–14 Don't waste too much time trying to get your own way at the moment, Leo! **21–22** Home and family are your priority now; this is a good time to organise a gathering to reminisce with others. **28–29** A time of peak physical energy when you should put your best foot forward in all work-related matters. **KEY DATES: HIGHS 16–17** Important actions should achieve good results, especially if you need to approach someone in authority at work. **LOWS 3–4; 30** In a potentially insecure period, keep your expectations of life realistic to avoid disappointment.

JULY: MAIN TRENDS: 3–4 Hasty action could lead to some practical setbacks and prove your undoing in some way, so think before you make any move. **10–11** Concentrate on building upon recent plans and getting your financial affairs in good order. **22–23** With the Sun in your sign, what happens personally and professionally ought to be productive and rewarding. There may be more ways than one to make great progress. **KEY DATES: HIGHS 14–15** Expect the best from life during this excellent period for new initiatives. **LOWS 1–2; 27–29** You may feel a little overburdened so keep major plans and appointments on the back burner for now.

AUGUST: MAIN TRENDS: 6–7 The timing should be perfect for new ideas that can help you to break away from the past and try something innovative. **13–14** A positive atmosphere pervades relationships, bringing out your romantic and fun-loving side. **22–23** Big projects may meet with success as your energies are constructively channelled into work. **KEY DATES: HIGHS 10–11** You'll have the energy to deal with, and resolve, any problem at work today. **LOWS 24–25** If work goes slightly awry with inexplicable mishaps, stick to tried-and-tested methods.

SEPTEMBER: MAIN TRENDS: 5–6 Although you can get along with just about anyone now, your love life offers the most satisfaction and perhaps even cause for celebration. **9–10** Keep your eyes and ears open for significant news at work. Your energy is in plentiful supply now. **23–24** If you have an inspired new career plan don't be afraid to push yourself forward should you get the chance to advance it. **KEY DATES: HIGHS 7–8** Give careful thought to any new financial proposition that comes your way. **LOWS 21–22** A generally slow-paced phase, with things at work in a stop–start mode.

OCTOBER: MAIN TRENDS: 10–11 Charisma seems to be your middle name and you will almost certainly find yourself in the best and most interesting company. **23–24** Trends place the emphasis on your personal independence as you put things into perspective and identify the overall direction of your plan. **30–31** Get an early start – you have the potential to succeed and can accomplish much if you channel your energies. **KEY DATES: HIGHS 4–5; 31** You excel at taking the initiative so don't hang back in getting new plans under way. **LOWS 17–19** Accept that it may be difficult to concentrate at work and focus instead on resting as much as you can.

NOVEMBER: MAIN TRENDS: 11–12 You may be more sensitive and impressionable than usual today and this could lead to some deep discussions over an emotional matter. **16–17** Attend to any unfinished business in your personal affairs; you may find that some time and space to think things through works wonders. **22–23** Quick decisions made at this time could lead to professional success and extra responsibility. **KEY DATES: HIGHS 1; 27–28** Push your luck a little and proceed with confidence to achieve more than expected. **LOWS 14–15** Prepare for one or two obstacles to stand in your way, and don't expect too much from others either.

DECEMBER: MAIN TRENDS: 2–3 Don't be a doormat – it's true that your spirits may be dwindling so try to avoid heavy work and enjoy some quiet time. **14–15** Open your mind and reach out to the world – perhaps try taking a trip out somewhere; getting out and about leads to unexpected surprises. **21–22** Your ego should receive a boost today as trends indicate that you will receive a compliment from someone in your social circle. **KEY DATES: HIGHS 25–26** Positive trends will increase your confidence and help you to maximise your social and romantic opportunities. **LOWS 11–13** Keep things simple and uncomplicated and accept that not everyone shares your views.

VIRGO BORN PEOPLE
Birthdays: 24 August to 23 September inclusive
Planet: Mercury. Birthstone: Sardonyx. Lucky day: Wednesday

Keynote for the Year: *Knowledge is power this year – use it together with your communication skills to help you to make progress this year.*

JANUARY: MAIN TRENDS: 11–12 You may be in a position of influence at work, but things go best when you co-operate with others. **18–19** Advantages arise in your career as go-ahead trends predominate – keep abreast of news and views. **22–23** Trends favour your social life and also one-to-one relationships so try putting work aside if you can. **KEY DATES: HIGHS 5–7** A very positive influence allows you to burn the candle at both ends, get lots done and still have energy left for leisure! **LOWS 20–21** Some unhelpful news might require action just when you are feeling less than dynamic – don't put things off, but take them slowly.

FEBRUARY: MAIN TRENDS: 10–11 This is not a time when you should expect to have your own way in social situations. Try to remain cool under pressure. **18–19** Stay cool and avoid obstacles if you have to deal with people you find challenging. **20–21** You may feel under pressure to eliminate old situations that have gone stale or even broken down; don't let it get to you but seize the initiative! **KEY DATES: HIGHS 2–3** Your energy levels reach a peak and everything seems to go your way for a day or so. **LOWS 16–18** During this monthly lull, concentrate on issues that can be completed quickly and don't expect them all to go swimmingly.

MARCH: MAIN TRENDS: 6–7 A trend that may sharpen up your financial instincts; gunning for what you want may prove easier than usual. **17–18** Virgo can always afford to be more open-minded, and today especially a broad view could help you with a vital matter. **20–21** This influence may give a boost to an important business or family matter wherever financial support is required. **KEY DATES: HIGHS 1–2; 29–30** You should be busily on the go and getting the best from life. **LOWS 15–17** Reduce your commitments and, at the same time, keep your demands of others simple as well.

APRIL: MAIN TRENDS: 1–2 Beware – some projects may not be as well thought through as they should be. Avoid unreasonable ambitions. **20–21** A beneficial period for finances when you shouldn't be short of ingenious ideas; the time to make a move could be now. **23–24** Trends suggest that this could be a crucial period of professional accomplishment – make the most of it! **KEY DATES: HIGHS 25–26** A luckier time than of late when you should be able to persuade others to get on board with your plans. **LOWS 12–13** It may be difficult to retain control over all everyday affairs during this lacklustre phase.

MAY: MAIN TRENDS: 13–15 With a sense of self-confidence in the workplace you can use all your persuasive powers over others to achieve your objectives. **19–20** Domestic matters may predominate at this time and you may hear some good news about your home or a family member. **23–24** If you are in a relationship, your partner will play an especially significant role at this time and could help to towards a lucky break. **KEY DATES: HIGHS 22–23** Instigate new projects and someone may do you a surprising favour right now. **LOWS 9–11** Trends indicate that you may be let down by a colleague – go easy on yourself and ride out the trend.

JUNE: MAIN TRENDS: 13–14 Contact with a variety of people can be useful and rewarding so venture out and broaden your horizons right now. **21–22** In a socially uplifting period you may receive some invitations, particularly from new friends or neighbours. **29–30** A good period for work and career-related affairs when events may line up in your favour and help you advance. **KEY DATES: HIGHS 18–20** A planetary boost for Virgoans when you ought to be feeling on top of the world. If a risky situation arises, back your instincts. **LOWS 5–7** Prepare for a slightly dull period when you feel a little sluggish. Rest for a while and ride out the trend.

JULY: MAIN TRENDS: 1–2 The planetary focus falls on your social pleasures and love life so try to mark these dates in your diary for some fun. **10–11** Studies undertaken at this time should go well, and you should also be able to multi-task successfully. **22–23** Long-buried issues may resurface now and a little soul-searching can pay dividends. **KEY DATES: HIGHS 16–17** Further your potential by taking one or two small risks that may open up new doors. **LOWS 3–4** You will need patience with tedious everyday tasks. Try a couple of early nights.

AUGUST: MAIN TRENDS: 6–7 The life and soul of the party, you can expect a welcoming response from others, especially romantically. **14–15** Business may have to come before pleasure at this pressing time, although perhaps you can combine both effectively? **23–24** Personal life issues move from the superficial to the deep at this time, but don't assume you have all the answers yet; take time to listen to others. **KEY DATES: HIGHS 12–13** Certain issues of major importance may now come to fruition, and the results may be better than you'd expected. **LOWS 26–28** Not the most positive influence when it comes to getting ahead, but you benefit from your own company.

SEPTEMBER: MAIN TRENDS: 6–7 You may feel rather impatient and eager to push on with one task after another, but pace yourself and avoid hasty decisions. **11–12** Your instinct is to withdraw into your personal space but don't make this a means of escape. You may have good intuitive insights now. **25–26** Your horizons are broadened and financial matters may receive a shot in the arm – go for it! **KEY DATES: HIGHS 9–10** A period of dynamic action and a great time for new beginnings of any description. **LOWS 23–24** Objectivity is the best attitude during this phase along with rest and relaxation.

OCTOBER: MAIN TRENDS: 10–11 Happy to be at home, family interests may outweigh professional concerns now. **23–24** A significant time work-wise with good results coming together. A recent issue may benefit from a little good luck. **30–31** As new initiatives get the go-ahead, your ability and effectiveness are at a peak and it is easier than ever to get ahead in your chosen field. **KEY DATES: HIGHS 6–7** Put your best foot forward, especially if you get the opportunity to take the lead. **LOWS 20–21** It may seem now that competitors are getting ahead better than you but avoid the 'grass is greener' attitude – you are wise enough to know this is rarely the case.

NOVEMBER: MAIN TRENDS: 11–12 Get involved in communications now as the exchange of information and ideas may now be central to your success. **14–15** This influence paves the way for excitement socially or romantically and you use your charm when trying to get what you want. **22–23** Don't be concerned if each little job isn't fulfilled right now, trends will soon increase your energy levels once more. **KEY DATES: HIGHS 2–3; 29–30** You relate especially well to others as planetary influences favour group social gatherings. **LOWS 16–18** Take life easily for now and set aside ambitions for a day or two.

DECEMBER: MAIN TRENDS: 2–3 A highly nostalgic time: fulfillment comes where familiar faces are found and encounters with people from the past warm the heart. **12–13** Love life is positively highlighted in your chart and it seems likely you will be in most people's good books. **21–22** Trends boost your spirits and make you more extroverted than usual so enjoy your moment in the social limelight. **KEY DATES: HIGHS 1; 27–28** A plan may get the green light and you won't shy away from hard work when it comes to getting things done. **LOWS 14–15** Keep a low profile and accept that these days are not likely to be your most successful or rewarding time.

Andy Murray

© PA Images

Tennis star and British hero Andy Murray was born in Glasgow on 15 May 1987, with some sources quoting a time of 2.10 pm. Even if we do not rely on this time of birth, however, the important qualities necessary to ensure Andy's meteoric success on the court are immediately obvious in his birth chart. It takes more than strength and stamina to be an international athlete. Of course Andy has both of these, but a Virgo ascendant and his Sun in Taurus bestow on him an Earth-sign determination to succeed and, most important of all, the sort of stubbornness and refusal to admit defeat that are so absolutely important to his chosen career.

In many respects Andy Murray's chart shows him to be a very steady personality. The Taurean Sun makes him quiet, though with Venus in Aries he was never a pushover in the schoolyard. Mercury in Gemini indicates he could really let his hair down on occasions, although a guiding and very important brake from Taurus always brings him back to the matter at hand, which in his case is tennis. With a well-spread and extremely well-balanced birth chart, Andy is more than intelligent enough to be aware when something might not be right and he has sufficient flexibility to make whatever changes are necessary to get life back on track. Added to all of this we have a strong constitution with just the slightest indication of a simmering resentment – sometimes against himself – which makes it all the more likely he will fight on to the bitter end.

Andy Murray's progressed chart indicates that his glory days are far from over. We can expect more sterling performances at Wimbledon, though there does seem to be a slight chance of some minor but significant physical setbacks during 2018, which might mean that this does not turn out to be his most successful year on the circuit.

At home Andy Murray is a settled family man. His chart shows he is no jetsetter and although he travels willingly enough to pursue his career, home and family will always be important to him. When it eventually becomes impossible to be the best on the tennis court, Andy Murray will find another pinnacle to climb. It isn't out of the question that when that time comes we will see a different Andy emerging, someone who is more outspoken and who will pursue issues that are not strictly sporting in nature. Andy Murray cannot avoid striving for any goal that is important to him because to do so is written clearly and in capital letters throughout his astrological makeup. What's more, Andy may go on to have several children and it is likely that the Murray dynasty in sport will continue into the future.

JANUARY

For High Water add 5h 30m for Bristol, 4h 23m for Hull, 0h 43m for Leith; subtract 2h 21m for Dublin, 1h 26m for Greenock, 2h 29m for Liverpool.

D of M	D of W	Festivals, Events and Anniversaries	Sun at London Rises	Sun at London Sets	High Water at London Bridge am	High Water at London Bridge pm	Moon at London Rises	Moon at London Sets	Weather
			h m	h m	h m	h m	h m	h m	
1	M	New Year's Day	8:06	16:02	01 28	13 50	15:48	6:59	
2	Tu	Bank Holiday (Scotland)	8:06	16:03	02 22	14 44	16:54	8:05	
3	W	Martin Luther excomm. 1521	8:05	16:04	03 13	15 37	18:08	8:59	
4	Th	Yorkshire Ripper caught 1981	8:05	16:05	04 02	16 27	19:26	9:43	
5	F	Tonghai earthquake 1970	8:05	16:06	04 48	17 16	20:44	10:18	
6	Sa	Epiphany	8:04	16:07	05 33	18 05	22:00	10:48	
7	Su	Galilei 4 Moons 1610	8:04	16:09	00 32	18 53	23:13	11:13	
8	M	Peter Sarstedt d. 2017	8:04	16:10	07 03	19 43	—	11:36	
9	Tu	Duchess of Cambridge b. 1982	8:03	16:11	07 53	20 35	0:23	11:59	
10	W	George Foreman b. 1949	8:03	16:13	08 51	21 29	1:31	12:22	
11	Th	Earhart solo flight 1935	8:02	16:14	09 54	22 28	2:37	12:48	
12	F	Graham Taylor d. 2017	8:01	16:16	10 59	23 35	3:41	13:16	
13	Sa	Labour Party first mtg 1893	8:01	16:17	—	12 06	4:42	13:48	
14	Su	First Gallup poll 1937	8:00	16:19	00 40	13 05	5:40	14:26	
15	M	Gamal Nasser b. 1918	7:59	16:20	01 33	13 56	6:34	15:11	
16	Tu	British Museum opened 1759	7:58	16:22	02 17	14 40	7:21	16:02	
17	W	Benjamin Franklin b. 1706	7:57	16:23	02 56	15 19	8:02	16:58	
18	Th	Cook disc. Hawaii 1778	7:56	16:25	03 30	15 54	8:37	17:59	
19	F	Edgar Allen Poe b. 1809	7:55	16:27	04 03	16 26	9:08	19:03	
20	Sa	Trump inauguration 2017	7:54	16:28	04 34	16 59	9:34	20:09	
21	Su	Monte Carlo rally 1911	7:53	16:30	05 06	17 33	9:59	21:17	
22	M	Sir Alf Ramsey b. 1920	7:52	16:32	05 39	18 09	10:21	22:26	
23	Tu	*Mise of Amiens* 1264	7:51	16:33	06 14	18 48	10:44	23:36	
24	W	Winston Churchill d. 1965	7:50	16:35	06 53	19 31	11:08	—	
25	Th	Burns Night	7:48	16:37	07 38	20 23	11:34	0:49	
26	F	Australia Day	7:47	16:39	08 33	21 30	12:06	2:04	
27	Sa	Holocaust Memorial Day	7:46	16:40	09 51	22 48	12:43	3:19	
28	Su	Seat belts law in UK 1983	7:44	16:42	11 18	—	13:31	4:34	
29	M	*The Raven* pub. 1845	7:43	16:44	00 02	12 31	14:29	5:42	
30	Tu	Gandhi assassinated 1948	7:42	16:46	01 11	13 38	15:38	6:42	
31	W	Total lunar eclise (10 51)	7:40	16:48	02 10	14 36	16:55	7:32	

Weather (vertical): Northerly winds will extend periods of snow, sleet and rain along with, mostly brief, bright and sunny intervals. Calmer and foggy conditions follow, colder mid-month, windy at close.

MOON'S PHASES JANUARY 2018			Days	Hours	Mins
	○	Full Moon	2	02	24
	☾	Last Quarter	8	22	25
	●	New Moon	17	02	17
	☽	First Quarter	24	22	20
	○	Full Moon	31	13	26

All times on this page are GMT

PREDICTIONS

The Full Moon on 2 January is in Cancer in a difficult opposition to Venus and Pluto and a harmonious grand trine to Mars and Neptune. Public opinion is exceptionally volatile and there is a high chance of by-elections or cabinet resignations within months. A New Year cabinet reshuffle could see a refreshing of the government. There will be announcements of increased spending on rail and transport projects. Global tensions centre on security fears over Pakistan's nuclear programme and border tensions with Afghanistan and India.

The New Moon on 17 January is in Capricorn in a conjunction with Venus and a challenging square to Uranus. Mars and Jupiter are rising at London. The latest technology will now revolutionise transport and worldwide connections. New medical technology will help ease bed shortages by allowing for remote consultations and surgery. The crisis in Europe is still intense, and the risk of fragmentation reaches a new high. Greece is in a renewed state of political turmoil. It is possible that at least one country will be following the UK in leaving the EU. Brexit negotiations could be going through a very bitter phase.

A second Full Moon of the month occurs on 31 January in Leo in an opposition to Venus.

An outsider may be the surprise victor at the Cheltenham *New Year Meeting*. The *Clarence House* Chase may be won by an 8-year-old.

FEBRUARY

For High Water add 5h 30m for Bristol, 4h 23m for Hull,
0h 43m for Leith; subtract 2h 21m for Dublin,
1h 26m for Greenock, 2h 29m for Liverpool.

D of M	D of W	Festivals, Events and Anniversaries	Sun at London Rises	Sun at London Sets	High Water at London Bridge am	High Water at London Bridge pm	Moon at London Rises	Moon at London Sets	Weather
			h m	h m	h m	h m	h m	h m	
1	Th	Labour Exchanges op. 1910	7:38	16:49	03 02	15 28	18:14	8:12	A change to milder weather with some sunny periods, although a further cold spell is likely to begin around or after mid-month when easterly wind with bring heavy frost and snowfall.
2	F	Candlemas Day	7:37	16:51	03 49	16 16	19:34	8:45	
3	Sa	Mendelssohn b. 1809	7:35	16:53	04 33	17 01	20:51	9:13	
4	Su	Radium E produced 1936	7:34	16:55	05 14	17 45	22:05	9:38	
5	M	Bakelite invented 1909	7:32	16:57	05 54	18 26	23:16	10:02	
6	Tu	Access. Elizabeth II 1952	7:30	16:58	06 34	19 07	—	10:26	
7	W	Pinocchio premiere 1940	7:29	17:00	07 15	19 48	0:24	10:51	
8	Th	Russo-Japan war beg. 1904	7:27	17:02	08 01	20 33	1:30	11:18	
9	F	Winter Olympics open	7:25	17:04	08 59	21 28	2:33	11:49	
10	Sa	Darnley murder 1567	7:23	17:06	10 09	22 35	3:33	12:25	
11	Su	Vatican City established 1929	7:22	17:08	11 23	23 56	4:28	13:07	
12	M	Charles Darwin b. 1809	7:20	17:09	12 35	—	5:17	13:56	
13	Tu	Shrove Tuesday	7:18	17:11	01 03	13 33	6:01	14:40	
14	W	St Valentine/Ash Wed	7:16	17:13	01 53	14 20	6:38	15:50	
15	Th	Partial solar eclipse (18 55)	7:14	17:15	02 35	15 00	7:10	16:54	
16	F	Chinese New Year	7:12	17:17	03 11	15 35	7:38	18:00	
17	Sa	Richard Briers d. 2013	7:10	17:19	03 45	16 08	8:04	19:08	
18	Su	Pluto discovered 1930	7:08	17:20	04 16	16 40	8:27	20:17	
19	M	Duke of York b. 1960	7:06	17:22	04 47	17 13	8:50	21:28	
20	Tu	Jimmy Greaves b. 1920	7:04	17:24	05 20	17 47	9:13	22:39	
21	W	Identity cards abolished 1952	7:02	17:26	05 54	18 24	9:38	23:52	
22	Th	N. Rock nationalised 2008	7:00	17:28	06 32	19 04	10:07	—	
23	F	Samuel Pepys b. 1633	6:58	17:29	07 16	19 52	10:41	1:06	
24	Sa	Dennis Waterman b. 1946	6:56	17:31	08 10	20 53	11:23	2:19	
25	Su	Winter Olympics close	6:54	17:33	09 24	22 15	12:14	3:27	
26	M	Fanny Cradock b. 1909	6:52	17:35	10 57	23 42	13:17	4:29	
27	Tu	Reichstag fire 1933	6:50	17:37	—	12 19	14:28	5:21	
28	W	First Gulf War ends 1991	6:48	17:38	00 59	13 31	15:45	6:05	

MOON'S PHASES FEBRUARY 2018			Days	Hours	Mins
	☾	Last Quarter	7	15	53
	●	New Moon	15	21	05
	☽	First Quarter	23	08	09

All times on this page are GMT

PREDICTIONS

The Month begins in the wake of the eclipsed Full Moon in Leo, which falls in the third house at London in a wide square to Jupiter. This could be a moment of hope and inspiration. New legal decisions should strengthen the rights of women in the workplace. There will be developments in mining for rare minerals, bringing depressed areas back to life. We may also see advances in fracking and the discovery of new oil reserves in the North Sea, holding out the promise of an end to fears of decline.

The New Moon on 15 February falls in Aquarius and is an eclipse in a square to Jupiter and semi-sextile to Uranus. There could be a leadership challenge in the Labour Party, along with renewed uncertainty. The eclipse is conjunct the USA's Moon which points to a very difficult and unpredictable period for American democracy in the build up to the mid-term elections. All economic indicators are rising and there is a high chance both of increased inflation, a rising stock-market and rising unemployment, with an all-round sense of instability. There could be a crisis in Panama, with American troops active in the canal zone.

A 6-year-old may romp home in this month's *Betfair Ascot Chase*, while a 7-year-old carrying 11st 1lb may win the *Betfair Hurdle* at Newbury.

MARCH

For High Water add 5h 30m for Bristol, 4h 23m for Hull, 0h 43m for Leith; subtract 2h 21m for Dublin, 1h 26m for Greenock, 2h 29m for Liverpool.

D of M	D of W	Festivals, Events and Anniversaries	Sun at London Rises	Sun at London Sets	High Water at London Bridge am	High Water at London Bridge pm	Moon at London Rises	Moon at London Sets	Weather
			h m	h m	h m	h m	h m	h m	
1	Th	St David's Day	6:45	17:40	01 59	14 27	17:04	6:40	
2	F	D H Lawrence d. 1930	6:43	17:42	02 48	15 15	18:23	7:11	
3	Sa	Carmen op. Paris 1875	6:41	17:44	03 31	15 59	19:40	7:37	
4	Su	Forth Bridge op. 1890	6:39	17:45	04 11	16 39	20:54	8:02	
5	M	Boston Massacre 1770	6:37	17:47	04 49	17 18	22:05	8:26	
6	Tu	Louisa M. Alcott d. 1888	6:35	17:49	05 27	17 54	23:14	8:51	
7	W	Bell telephone patent 1876	6:32	17:51	06 03	18 28	—	9:18	
8	Th	Kenneth Grahame b. 1859	6:30	17:52	06 41	19 03	0:20	9:47	
9	F	Barbie doll debuts 1959	6:28	17:54	07 21	19 42	1:22	10:22	
10	Sa	Prince Edward b. 1964	6:26	17:56	08 11	20 32	2:20	11:02	
11	Su	Mothering Sunday	6:23	17:58	09 20	21 42	3:12	11:48	
12	M	Liza Minnelli b. 1946	6:21	17:59	10 41	23 09	3:57	12:40	
13	Tu	Commonwealth Day	6:19	18:01	11 59	—	4:37	13:38	
14	W	Albert Einstein b. 1879	6:17	18:03	00 26	13 02	5:11	14:41	
15	Th	Julius Caesar assass. 44 BC	6:14	18:04	01 21	13 51	5:40	15:46	
16	F	Harold Wilson resigns 1976	6:12	18:06	02 06	14 32	6:07	16:55	
17	Sa	St Patrick's Day	6:10	18:08	02 44	15 08	6:31	18:04	
18	Su	Last debutantes 1957	6:08	18:10	03 18	15 42	6:54	19:16	
19	M	Sydney Harbour Br. op. 1932	6:05	18:11	03 51	16 15	7:17	20:29	
20	Tu	Vernal equinox 16 15	6:03	18:13	04 25	16 50	7:42	21:43	
21	W	Poll tax riot 1990	6:01	18:15	04 59	17 25	8:10	22:57	
22	Th	William Shatner b. 1931	5:59	18:16	05 36	18 02	8:42	—	
23	F	Roger Bannister b. 1929	5:56	18:18	06 15	18 42	9:21	0:11	
24	Sa	Alan Sugar b. 1947	5:54	18:20	07 01	19 30	10:09	1:20	
25	Su	Palm Sunday	5:52	18:21	07 58	20 31	11:06	2:23	
26	M	First Henley Regatta 1839	5:49	18:23	09 15	21 55	12:12	3:17	
27	Tu	Yuri Gagarin d. 1968	5:47	18:25	10 46	23 28	13:25	4:02	
28	W	Michael Parkinson b. 1935	5:45	18:26	—	12 10	14:42	4:39	
29	Th	EU Article 50 invoked 2017	5:43	18:28	00 45	13 19	15:59	6:10	
30	F	Good Friday/Passover	5:40	18:30	01 42	14 12	17:16	5:37	
31	Sa	John Christie arrested 1953	5:38	18:31	02 28	21 36	18:31	6:02	

Weather column (vertical text): Traditional March winds are in evidence, easterly and northerly but becoming damper (south to west) by the third week. The surprise of some warm sunny weather at the close will be welcome.

			Days	Hours	Mins
MOON'S	○	Full Moon	2	00	51
PHASES	☾	Last Quarter	9	11	19
MARCH	●	New Moon	17	13	11
2018	☽	First Quarter	24	15	35
	○	Full Moon	31	12	26

All times on this page are GMT (Add 1 hr BST from 25th)

PREDICTIONS

The first Full Moon of the month occurs on 2 March in Virgo. Government popularity will be in free-fall but the opposition will be disorganised, opening the way for minority parties. Disputes at sea will be based around fishing. Expect a new 'cod-war'. The global situation will be afflicted by renewed confusion. Low-lying areas are at risk from tidal waves. Attention turns to Southeast Asia. The eclipse falls on the Indonesian Midheaven, pointing to political upheaval, street protests and a threat to stability. Papua New Guinea is at risk from floods or tsunamis. Vietnam will assert itself as a leading super-power, and is heading for a military stand-off with China.

The New Moon on 17 March is in Pisces conjunct the fixed star Scheat, a square to Mars and a trine to Jupiter. In spite of high hopes, new enterprises which are launched now could sink without trace. Entrepreneurs are advised to pay careful attention to detail and accept delay where necessary. Children's rights are top of the agenda in legal cases. Expect violent storms and tornadoes as the weather turns volatile in the American Midwest.

The second Full Moon falls on 31 March in Libra, in a tough 'T' square with Mars and Saturn.

The winner at this year's *Cheltenham Gold Cup* could be a 10-year-old 2nd favourite. Meanwhile, Sandown's *Imperial Cup* may be won by a 5-year-old horse carrying 10 st 11lb.

APRIL

For High Water add 5h 30m for Bristol, 4h 23m for Hull, 0h 43m for Leith; subtract 2h 21m for Dublin, 1h 26m for Greenock, 2h 29m for Liverpool.

D of M	D of W	Festivals, Events and Anniversaries	Sun at London Rises	Sun at London Sets	High Water at London Bridge am	High Water at London Bridge pm	Moon at London Rises	Moon at London Sets	Weather
			h m	h m	h m	h m	h m	h m	
1	Su	Easter Sunday	5:36	18:33	03 08	15 36	19:44	6:26	After a fine start, showers will predominate, changing by the third week to mostly fine weather typical of a fine spring in the south, but cooler, showery and some snow in the north and east.
2	M	Easter Monday	5:33	18:35	03 46	16 13	20:55	6:50	
3	Tu	Prince Ranier d. 2005	5:31	18:36	04 23	16 47	22:04	7:16	
4	W	M Luther King assass. 1968	5:29	18:38	04 59	17 21	23:09	7:45	
5	Th	Churchill resigns 1955	5:27	18:40	05 35	17 53	—	8:17	
6	F	Sir John Betjeman b. 1906	5:24	18:41	06 11	18 24	12:10	8:55	
7	Sa	Vesuvius erupts 1906	5:22	18:43	06 48	18 59	1:05	9:39	
8	Su	Low Sunday	5:20	18:45	07 31	19 43	1:53	10:29	
9	M	Henry V crowned 1413	5:18	18:46	08 30	20 46	2:35	11:25	
10	Tu	Evelyn Waugh d. 1966	5:16	18:48	09 55	22 19	3:11	12:25	
11	W	*Apollo 13* launched 1970	5:13	18:50	11 14	23 40	3:42	13:30	
12	Th	Franklin D. Roosevelt d. 1945	5:11	18:52	—	12 19	4:09	14:37	
13	F	Guy Fawkes b. 1570	5:09	18:53	00 40	13 12	4:33	15:46	
14	Sa	Sir John Gielgud b. 1904	5:07	18:55	01 28	13 56	4:56	16:58	
15	Su	Hillsborough disaster 1989	5:05	18:57	02 08	14 34	5:19	18:11	
16	M	Spike Milligan b. 1918	5:03	18:58	02 46	15 12	5:44	19:27	
17	Tu	Billy Fury b. 1940	5:00	19:00	03 24	15 49	6:10	20:43	
18	W	San Francisco 'quake 1906	4:58	19:02	04 02	16 27	6:41	22:00	
19	Th	Dame Kelly Holmes b. 1970	4:56	19:03	04 41	17 06	7:18	23:13	
20	F	Powell *Rivers Of Blood* 1968	4:54	19:05	05 21	17 45	8:04	—	
21	Sa	HM the Queen b. 1926	4:52	19:07	06 05	18 28	8:59	12:19	
22	Su	Vladimir Lenin b. 1870	4:50	19:08	06 54	19 18	10:03	1:16	
23	M	St George's Day	4:48	19:10	07 56	20 22	11:14	2:04	
24	Tu	Sweets rationing ended 1949	4:46	19:12	09 15	21 46	12:28	2:42	
25	W	Anzac Day	4:44	19:13	10 35	23 09	13:44	3:14	
26	Th	Sid James d. 1976	4:42	19:15	11 52	—	14:59	3:41	
27	F	Pope J Paul II canonized 2014	4:40	19:17	00 21	12 58	16:13	4:06	
28	Sa	Wembley Stadium op. 1923	4:38	19:18	01 18	13 50	17:26	4:26	
29	Su	Chernobyl disaster 1986	4:36	19:20	02 04	14 33	18:38	4:52	
30	M	Hitler's suicide 1945	4:34	19:21	02 44	15 11	19:47	6:16	

MOON'S PHASES APRIL 2018			Days	Hours	Mins
	☾	Last Quarter	8	07	17
	●	New Moon	16	01	57
	☽	First Quarter	22	21	45
	○	Full Moon	30	00	58

All times on this page are GMT (Add 1 hr BST)

PREDICTIONS

The month opens with a tough, uncompromising 'T Square' between the Sun, Mercury, Mars and Saturn. The UK is at risk from re-energised pressure for Scottish independence. This is the most dangerous moment of the year for European unity and global stability. China will be flexing its military muscles in the South China Sea, but the government may also be facing stiff opposition at home as discontent builds up. Elsewhere, planning laws will be relaxed in order to encourage new transport links. The international drug war will be declared over by the UN, although the UK will toughen its anti-drug stance.

The New Moon on 16 April is in Aries in a conjunction with Uranus and a square to Mars and Pluto. Global tension remains sky high. The international situation is revolutionary. A series of countries including Morocco, Algeria, Spain, France and Germany are at risk from civil strife. The Baltic States will be under pressure from Russia and could be a potential flashpoint between East and West. Parts of Nigeria are on the brink of civil war between religious factions.

The Full Moon on 30 April is in Scorpio in the ninth house at London. Mars and Pluto are rising, causing instability as May begins.

An 11-year-old favourite may be victorious at Aintree this year in the *Grand National* meeting, while the *Scottish National* may go to a 9-year-old.

MAY

For High Water add 5h 30m for Bristol, 4h 23m for Hull, 0h 43m for Leith; subtract 2h 21m for Dublin, 1h 26m for Greenock, 2h 29m for Liverpool.

D of M	D of W	Festivals, Events and Anniversaries	Sun at London Rises	Sun at London Sets	High Water London Bridge am	High Water London Bridge pm	Moon at London Rises	Moon at London Sets	Wea- ther
			h m	h m	h m	h m	h m	h m	
1	Tu	Ayrton Senna killed 1994	4:32	19:23	03 21	15 45	20:55	5:43	
2	W	Princess Charlotte b. 2015	4:30	19:25	03 58	16 19	21:58	6:14	
3	Th	First heart transplant 1968	4:28	19:26	04 34	16 51	22:56	6:50	
4	F	Star Wars day	4:27	19:28	05 10	17 22	23:48	7:31	
5	Sa	Napolean d. 1821	4:25	19:30	05 46	17 54	—	8:19	
6	Su	Rogation Sunday	4:23	19:31	06 21	18 27	0:33	9:12	
7	M	Bank holiday	4:21	19:33	07 02	19 09	1:11	10:11	
8	Tu	World Red Cross day	4:20	19:34	07 52	20 02	1:43	11:13	
9	W	Lawn mower patented 1899	4:18	19:36	09 00	21 16	2:11	12:19	
10	Th	Ascension Day	4:16	19:38	10 21	22 45	2:36	13:26	
11	F	Spencer Perceval assass. 1812	4:15	19:39	11 27	23 50	2:59	14:36	
12	Sa	Burt Bacharach b. 1928	4:13	19:41	—	12 24	3:22	15:48	
13	Su	Paris student riots 1968	4:11	19:42	00 43	13 14	3:45	17:03	
14	M	State of Israel est. 1948	4:10	19:44	01 30	13 59	4:10	18:20	
15	Tu	First day of Ramadan	4:08	19:45	02 15	14 43	4:39	19:39	
16	W	Jim Henson d. 1990	4:07	19:47	02 59	15 26	5:13	20:56	
17	Th	Dennis Hopper b. 1936	4:06	19:48	03 43	16 09	5:56	22:08	
18	F	Mt St Helens erupts 1980	4:04	19:50	11 09	16 52	6:49	23:11	
19	Sa	Shavuot begins	4:03	19:51	05 13	17 35	7:51	—	
20	Su	Pentecost	4:01	19:53	06 01	18 21	9:02	0:04	
21	M	Cutty Sark fire 2007	4:00	19:54	06 55	19 13	10:17	0:45	
22	Tu	Arthur Conan Doyle b. 1859	3:59	19:55	07 57	20 17	11:33	1:19	
23	W	Bonnie and Clyde killed 1934	3:58	19:57	09 06	21 31	12:49	1:48	
24	Th	Queen Victoria b. 1819	3:57	19:58	10 15	22 43	14:02	2:12	
25	F	Diet of Worms ends 1521	3:55	19:59	11 24	23 50	15:14	2:35	
26	Sa	Petrol rationing ended 1950	3:54	20:01	—	12 30	16:25	2:57	
27	Su	King John crowned 1199	3:53	20:02	00 49	13 23	17:35	3:21	
28	M	Spring Bank Holiday	3:52	20:03	01 38	14 08	18:43	3:46	
29	Tu	Wesak Day	3:51	20:04	02 21	14 47	19:47	4:14	
30	W	Airbus A300 in service 1974	3:50	20:05	03 00	15 22	20:48	4:47	
31	Th	Corpus Christi	3:50	20:07	03 38	15 55	22:43	5:26	

Weather column note: Generally cool at the start with overnight frost, improving with spring sunshine and warmth. Some record high temperatures during the final ten days may lead to localised freak storms.

MOON'S PHASES MAY 2018		Days	Hours	Mins
☾	Last Quarter	8	02	08
●	New Moon	15	11	47
☽	First Quarter	22	03	49
○	Full Moon	29	14	19

All times on this page are GMT (Add 1 hr BST)

PREDICTIONS

May opens with a planetary square between Mars and Pluto and Uranus. This is a highly confrontational situation and levels of global tension remain high. The UK is still very unstable with high levels of discontent in every sector of society. Political opinion becomes ever-more polarised and the break-up of the UK is a real fear. Scandinavia is also at risk of political upheaval. There could be a new hard-line government in Iran and changes at the top of government in Iraq.

The New Moon on 15 May is in Taurus in the tenth house at London, and a trine to Mars and Pluto. House prices are stagnant or dropping, and it's a buyers' market. New art and music movements seize the public imagination and create a new, positive, cultural mood.

The Full Moon on 29 May is in Sagittarius. Venus is on the Midheaven at London, in an opposition to Saturn and grand trine with Jupiter and Neptune. This is a moment of great romantic inspiration, perfect for dreamers, mystics and artists. The government announces further major building plans in order to ease the housing shortage. International tension begins to drop and against this backdrop it is increasingly possible to look forward to a brighter, better world and an exciting future.

The *2,000 Guineas* at Newmarket (open to 3-year-olds only) could be won by an Irish jockey, whereas the *1,000 Guineas* may go to an outsider.

JUNE

For High Water add 5h 30m for Bristol, 4h 23m for Hull, 0h 43m for Leith; subtract 2h 21m for Dublin, 1h 26m for Greenock, 2h 29m for Liverpool.

D of M	D of W	Festivals, Events and Anniversaries	Sun at London Rises	Sun at London Sets	High Water at London Bridge am	High Water at London Bridge pm	Moon at London Rises	Moon at London Sets	Wea-ther
			h m	h m	h m	h m	h m	h m	
1	F	Marilyn Monroe b. 1926	3:49	20:08	04 15	16 27	22:30	6:11	Above-average sunshine and temperatures across Britain, barring a few short thunderstorms in the south and east and local rain. Almost certain to be the best month for summer holidays.
2	Sa	Feast of St Elmo	3:48	20:09	04 51	16 59	23:11	7:03	
3	Su	Muhammad Ali d. 2016	3:47	20:10	05 26	17 32	23:45	7:59	
4	M	Kaiser Wilhelm II d. 1941	3:47	20:11	06 01	18 06	—	9:00	
5	Tu	Feast of St Boniface	3:46	20:12	06 40	18 46	0:15	10:04	
6	W	Bjorn Borg b. 1956	3:45	20:13	07 25	19 32	0:40	11:09	
7	Th	Christopher Lee d. 2015	3:45	20:13	08 18	20 27	1:03	12:17	
8	F	Prophet Muhammad d. 632	3:44	20:14	09 26	21 42	1:25	13:26	
9	Sa	Gatwick Airport opened 1958	3:44	20:15	10 35	22 58	1:47	14:39	
10	Su	Duke of Edinburgh b. 1921	3:43	20:16	11 37	—	2:10	15:54	
11	M	USS *Missouri* comm. 1944	3:43	20:17	00 00	12 35	2:36	17:11	
12	Tu	Gregory Peck d. 2003	3:43	20:17	00 56	13 29	3:07	18:30	
13	W	Kathy Burke b. 1964	3:43	20:18	01 48	14 19	3:46	19:47	
14	Th	End of Ramadan (Eid al-Fitr)	3:42	20:18	02 39	15 08	4:34	20:56	
15	F	The Black Prince b. 1330	3:42	20:19	03 28	15 55	5:34	21:56	
16	Sa	Screaming Ld Sutch d. 1999	3:42	20:19	04 18	16 42	6:43	22:44	
17	Su	Father's Day	3:42	20:20	05 07	17 28	8:00	23:22	
18	M	Autistic Pride Day	3:42	20:20	05 58	18 15	9:18	23:52	
19	Tu	Boris Johnson b. 1964	3:42	20:20	06 50	19 05	10:36	—	
20	W	*Jaws* released 1975	3:42	20:21	07 46	20 02	11:52	0:19	
21	Th	Summer solstice (11 07)	3:43	20:21	08 45	21 05	13:05	0:42	
22	F	Feast of St Thomas More	3:43	20:21	09 46	22 10	14:16	1:04	
23	Sa	UK votes to leave EU 2016	3:43	20:21	10 49	23 14	15:26	1:27	
24	Su	UK Armed Forces Day	3:43	20:21	11 54	—	16:33	1:51	
25	M	Korean War began 1950	3:44	20:21	00 16	12 53	17:39	3:18	
26	Tu	V&A Museum opened 1909	3:44	20:21	01 12	13 43	18:41	3:48	
27	W	Stratford Martyrs exec. 1556	3:45	20:21	02 00	14 25	19:37	3:25	
28	Th	Treaty of Versailles 1919	3:45	20:21	02 44	15 03	20:28	4:07	
29	F	Globe theatre fire 1613	3:46	20:21	03 24	15 38	21:11	4:56	
30	Sa	Stanley Spencer b. 1891	3:46	20:21	04 02	16 11	21:47	5:51	

MOON'S PHASES JUNE 2018			Days	Hours	Mins
	☾	Last Quarter	6	18	31
	●	New Moon	13	19	43
	☽	First Quarter	20	10	50
	○	Full Moon	28	04	53

All times on this page are GMT (Add 1 hr BST)

PREDICTIONS

The New Moon on 13 June falls in Gemini in the seventh house at London. Mercury is opposed to Saturn. Worldwide it is time for tough negotiations to resolve long-forgotten conflicts. It is now necessary to look at all points of view, and enemies must talk to each other. The scandal-hit South African government may fall after a corruption scandal. There is danger at sea and a global risk of floods and tidal waves. Disease epidemics could result from ill-judged health cuts. There are concerns of a spike in the divorce rate. This month's key legal cases concern unsuccessful attempts to roll back rights for gay and transgender people.

The Full Moon on 28 June falls in Capricorn in a conjunction with Saturn. Reorganisation in the Health Service will reverse recent reforms and focus on traditional solutions, such as matrons and extended local services. International tension increases, although governments will be looking for sensible, practical collaboration rather than conflict. War is off the agenda. Chinese trade with the rest of the world increases and markets benefit from a brief 'peace dividend'. Foreign policy blunders embarrass the British government. Government ministers may be caught up in a bribery scandal.

At the Epsom *Oaks* this year, victory should go to a well-backed favourite, while the *Derby* may be won by a Midlands-born jockey.

Government
Change

JULY

For High Water add 5h 30m for Bristol, 4h 23m for Hull,
0h 43m for Leith; subtract 2h 21m for Dublin,
1h 26m for Greenock, 2h 29m for Liverpool.

D of M	D of W	Festivals, Events and Anniversaries	Sun at London Rises	Sun at London Sets	High Water at London Bridge am	High Water at London Bridge pm	Moon at London Rises	Moon at London Sets	Weather
			h m	h m	h m	h m	h m	h m	
1	Su	Princess Diana b. 1961	3:47	20:20	04 36	16 43	22:18	6:51	The generally fine weather continues, although with thundery interludes and some freak winds both early and later in the month, when conditions vary. Rain should seldom be prolonged.
2	M	Battle of Marston Moor 1644	3:48	20:20	05 10	17 15	22:45	7:53	
3	Tu	Jim Morrison d. 1971	3:49	20:20	05 44	17 49	23:08	8:58	
4	W	US Independence Day	3:49	20:19	06 20	18 25	23:30	10:04	
5	Th	Bikini on sale 1946	3:50	20:19	06 59	19 04	23:51	11:11	
6	F	Piper Alpha disaster 1988	3:51	20:18	07 44	19 49	—	12:20	
7	Sa	7/7 terrorist attacks 2005	3:52	20:17	08 37	20 46	0:13	13:32	
8	Su	R Biggs escaped 1965	3:53	20:17	09 45	22 03	0:37	14:46	
9	M	Sir Edward Heath b. 1916	3:54	20:16	10 55	23 20	1:04	16:03	
10	Tu	*News Of The Wld* closed 2011	3:55	20:15	—	12 00	1:38	17:20	
11	W	Waterloo station op. 1848	3:56	20:15	00 26	13 03	2:20	18:33	
12	Th	Orangemen's Day (hol) NI	3:57	20:14	01 26	14 00	3:13	19:39	
13	F	Partial solar eclipse (01 48)	3:58	20:13	02 23	14 53	4:18	20:33	
14	Sa	Bastille Day (France)	3:59	20:12	03 17	15 43	5:34	21:17	
15	Su	St Swithin's Day	4:00	20:11	04 08	16 30	6:54	21:52	
16	M	Barbara Stanwyck b. 1907	4:02	20:10	04 58	17 19	8:15	22:21	
17	Tu	Angela Merkel b. 1954	4:03	20:09	05 46	18 00	9:35	22:46	
18	W	Spanish Civil War began 1936	4:04	20:08	06 34	18 45	10:51	23:10	
19	Th	Paris Metro op. 1900	4:05	20:07	07 23	19 34	12:05	23:32	
20	F	International Chess Day	4:07	20:05	08 14	20 28	13:16	23:56	
21	Sa	Ernest Hemingway b. 1899	4:08	20:04	09 07	21 28	14:24	—	
22	Su	Prince George b. 2013	4:09	20:03	10 05	22 32	15:31	0:22	
23	M	Amy Winehouse d. 2011	4:11	20:02	11 09	23 40	16:34	0:51	
24	Tu	Peter Sellers d. 1980	4:12	20:00	—	12 18	17:32	1:25	
25	W	First test tube baby 1978	4:13	19:59	00 45	13 17	18:24	2:05	
26	Th	Carl Jung b. 1875	4:15	19:57	01 41	14 05	19:10	2:52	
27	F	Total lunar eclipse (17 14)	4:16	19:56	02 28	14 46	19:49	3:45	
28	Sa	Beatrix Potter b. 1866	4:18	19:54	03 10	15 22	20:22	4:43	
29	Su	Charles and Diana m. 1981	4:19	19:53	03 47	15 55	20:49	5:45	
30	M	Frances de la Tour b. 1944	4:21	19:51	04 20	16 26	21:14	6:49	
31	Tu	Dr Crippen arrested 1910	4:22	19:50	04 52	16 57	21:36	7:55	

MOON'S PHASES JULY 2018			Days	Hours	Mins
	☾	Last Quarter	6	07	50
	●	New Moon	13	02	47
	☽	First Quarter	19	21	52
	○	Full Moon	27	20	20

All times on this page are GMT (Add 1 hr BST)

PREDICTIONS

The New Moon on 13 July is an eclipse in Cancer in an opposition to Pluto and a trine to Neptune in the tenth house at London. There will be chaos in the government, with deep splits over the future of the country's relationship with Europe. The economy is generally in an inflationary phase, but there are fears that a speculative bubble is building up, and of a future crash. Russia should avoid complacency as a major challenge to the government is now building. Under volatile trends, France is at risk from riots and civil disturbance.

The Full Moon on 27 July is an eclipse in Aquarius, in a conjunction with Mars in the twelfth house at London. This planetary picture indicates a high risk of espionage. Spy rings may be exposed and brought to light. A well-known bank may be on the brink of collapse after a major hacking scandal. Israel should have a new government and is heading for a change of direction. It is in an expansionary mood, and deepening its engagement in the Arab world. The notion of the 'Jewish' state may be called into question. East Africa is in a delicate position, and Kenya may be involved in a border war. There may be protests in Georgia.

At Ascot, a 5-year-old carrying 9st 7lb may win the *International Stakes*. A 4-year-old carrying 9st 2lb may win the *Darley July Cup* at Newmarket.

AUGUST

For High Water add 5h 30m for Bristol, 4h 23m for Hull, 0h 43m for Leith; subtract 2h 21m for Dublin, 1h 26m for Greenock, 2h 29m for Liverpool.

D of M	D of W	Festivals, Events and Anniversaries	Sun at London Rises	Sun at London Sets	High Water at London Bridge am	High Water at London Bridge pm	Moon at London Rises	Moon at London Sets	Weather
			h m	h m	h m	h m	h m	h m	
1	W	Berlin Olympics opened 1936	4:24	19:48	05 23	17 28	21:57	9:01	
2	Th	First US census 1790	4:25	19:46	05 56	18 01	22:18	10:09	
3	F	USS *Nautilus* North Pole 1958	4:27	19:45	06 32	18 37	22:40	11:18	
4	Sa	Percy Shelley b. 1792	4:28	19:43	07 11	19 18	23:05	12:29	
5	Su	Henry I crowned 1100	4:30	19:41	07 57	20 08	23:35	13:43	
6	M	Bank holiday (Scotland)	4:31	19:40	08 55	21 14	—	14:57	
7	Tu	Oliver Hardy d. 1957	4:33	19:38	10 12	22 44	0:11	16:10	
8	W	Esther Williams b. 1921	4:34	19:36	11 30	—	0:57	17:19	
9	Th	Whitney Houston b. 1963	4:36	19:34	00 01	12 42	1:55	18:18	
10	F	Treaty of Nonsuch 1585	4:37	19:32	01 10	13 45	3:05	19:07	
11	Sa	Partial solar eclipse (08 02)	4:39	19:30	02 12	14 39	4:24	19:47	
12	Su	Sewing machine pat. 1861	4:41	19:28	03 06	15 27	5:46	20:19	
13	M	Kenny Baker d. 2016	4:42	19:27	03 55	16 12	7:09	20:47	
14	Tu	Japan surrender 1945	4:44	19:25	04 41	16 55	8:29	21:12	
15	W	Princess Royal b. 1950	4:45	19:23	05 25	17 36	9:46	21:35	
16	Th	Margaret Mitchell d. 1949	4:47	19:21	06 08	18 17	11:00	21:59	
17	F	Mae West b. 1892	4:48	19:19	06 50	18 59	12:12	22:25	
18	Sa	*Lolita* published 1958	4:50	19:17	07 33	19 45	13:21	22:53	
19	Su	Helium discovered 1868	4:52	19:15	08 18	20 41	14:26	23:26	
20	M	Soviets invade Prague 1968	4:53	19:12	09 12	21 48	15:26	—	
21	Tu	Princess Margaret b. 1930	4:55	19:10	10 18	23 01	16:20	0:04	
22	W	1st Geneva Convention 1864	4:56	19:08	11 37	—	17:08	0:48	
23	Th	Marseille liberated 1944	4:58	19:06	00 16	12 47	17:49	1:39	
24	F	Ukraine independence 1991	5:00	19:04	01 18	13 39	18:24	2:36	
25	Sa	Richard III remains disc 2013	5:01	19:02	02 07	14 22	18:53	3:37	
26	Su	Macaulay Culkin b. 1980	5:03	19:00	02 48	14 59	19:19	4:41	
27	M	Summer bank holiday	5:04	18:58	03 24	15 32	19:41	5:46	
28	Tu	Philadelphia race riot 1964	5:06	18:55	03 57	16 03	20:03	6:53	
29	W	Gene Wilder d. 2016	5:08	18:53	04 27	16 33	20:23	8:01	
30	Th	Andy Roddick b. 1982	5:09	18:51	04 57	17 04	20:45	9:10	
31	F	Princess Diana d. 1997	5:11	18:49	05 30	17 37	21:09	10:20	

The best of the weather may be delayed until the second and third weeks, while early and late may be less settled, especially in the south and west. Temperatures at or above average.

MOON'S PHASES AUGUST 2018		Days	Hours	Mins
☾	Last Quarter	4	18	17
●	New Moon	11	09	57
☽	First Quarter	18	07	48
○	Full Moon	26	11	56

All times on this page are GMT (Add 1 hr BST)

PREDICTIONS

The New Moon on 11 August is an eclipse in Leo in the tenth house at London, in a conjunction with Mercury and a square with Jupiter. There will be calls for Parliament to be recalled to debate an emergency situation. Government debt will be increasing, and major technological investments are likely to massively overspend. Doubts are raised about the financial viability of nuclear energy. The Republic of Ireland is experiencing a summer boom, with rapidly rising property prices, a growing financial sector and scope for investment. Pakistan is due for a change of government which may alarm its Western allies.

The Full Moon on 26 August is an eclipse in Pisces, on the IC at London, and in a sextile to Saturn and Uranus. The Sun is on the Midheaven. In the UK, workplace rights are threatened and the government will clamp down on charities which break the law. Russia is in the midst of a democratic revival, and the government is riding a wave of popularity. In South Africa, the ANC government will finally collapse and may be replaced by a wider coalition, marking a major moment of transition, post-apartheid. The Palestinians will be seeking a reunion of the West Bank and the Gaza Strip.

In the *King George Stakes* at Goodwood a 4-year-old carrying 9st 2lb may be the winner, whilst in the *Ebor Handicap* at York a 5-year-old favourite carrying 9st 10lb may win.

SEPTEMBER

For High Water add 5h 30m for Bristol, 4h 23m for Hull, 0h 43m for Leith; subtract 2h 21m for Dublin, 1h 26m for Greenock, 2h 29m for Liverpool.

D of M	D of W	Festivals, Events and Anniversaries	Sun at London Rises	Sun at London Sets	High Water at London Bridge am	High Water at London Bridge pm	Moon at London Rises	Moon at London Sets	Weather
			h m	h m	h m	h m	h m	h m	
1	Sa	Hitler invaded Poland 1939	5:12	18:47	06 04	18 12	21:36	11:32	Settled weather should return following an uncertain start with some typically high late-summer temperatures to match. Warm and sunny days predominate, although windy at the close.
2	Su	Treaty of Jaffa 1192	5:14	18:44	06 41	18 53	22:09	12:44	
3	M	War declared 1939	5:16	18:42	07 24	19 42	22:49	13:56	
4	Tu	Steve Irwin d. 2006	5:17	18:40	08 18	20 46	23:41	15:04	
5	W	Freddie Mercury b. 1946	5:19	18:38	09 33	22 18	—	16:05	
6	Th	Sir Len Hutton d. 1990	5:20	18:35	11 04	23 44	0:43	16:57	
7	F	*Luisitania* md'n voyage 1907	5:22	18:33	—	12 25	1:56	17:40	
8	Sa	Severn Bridge opened 1966	5:24	18:31	00 59	13 30	3:16	18:15	
9	Su	Battle of Flodden 1513	5:25	18:29	02 00	14 22	4:38	18:45	
10	M	Jewish New Year	5:27	18:26	02 51	15 07	6:00	19:11	
11	Tu	9/11 2001	5:28	18:24	03 36	15 49	7:20	19:35	
12	W	Islamic New Year	5:30	18:22	04 18	16 29	8:38	19:59	
13	Th	Arafat/Rabin peace 1993	5:31	18:19	04 58	17 08	9:53	20:24	
14	F	Feast of The Cross	5:33	18:17	05 36	17 46	11:05	20:52	
15	Sa	Prince Harry b. 1984	5:35	18:15	06 13	18 25	12:13	21:23	
16	Su	Wall Street bombing 1920	5:36	18:12	06 49	19 07	13:17	22:00	
17	M	Damon Hill b. 1960	5:38	18:10	07 28	19 56	14:14	22:43	
18	Tu	Yom Kippur begins	5:39	18:08	08 16	21 02	15:05	23:32	
19	W	Jeremy Irons b. 1948	5:41	18:06	09 24	22 22	15:48	—	
20	Th	Premier League formed 1991	5:43	18:03	10 52	23 40	16:25	0:26	
21	F	*The Hobbit* pub. 1937	5:44	18:01	—	12 09	16:56	1:26	
22	Sa	Anne of Cleves b. 1515	5:46	17:59	00 46	13 05	17:22	2:29	
23	Su	Autumn equinox (02 54)	5:47	17:56	01 37	13 51	18:46	3:35	
24	M	2nd day of Sukkot	5:49	17:54	02 18	14 29	18:08	4:42	
25	Tu	Fletcher Christian b. 1764	5:51	17:52	02 54	15 02	18:29	5:50	
26	W	NZ became Dominion 1907	5:52	17:49	03 26	15 34	18:50	7:00	
27	Th	Jesuits founded 1540	5:54	17:47	03 57	16 05	19:13	8:11	
28	F	Shimon Peres d. 2016	5:56	17:45	04 30	16 39	19:39	9:23	
29	Sa	Michaelmas Day	5:57	17:43	05 03	17 14	20:09	10:36	
30	Su	Radio 1 launched 1967	5:59	17:40	05 38	17 52	20:47	11:48	

MOON'S PHASES SEPTEMBER 2018		Days	Hours	Mins
	☾ Last Quarter	3	02	37
	● New Moon	9	18	01
	☽ First Quarter	16	23	14
	○ Full Moon	25	02	52

All times on this page are GMT (Add 1 hr BST)

PREDICTIONS

The New Moon on 9 September is in Virgo in a trine to Pluto and an opposition to Neptune. Foreign negotiations will be resolved, but the UK will be in a weak position and will give way to demands by its rivals. The government may be subject to bitter attacks and leaks will smear at least one government minister. Investment in renewable energy, including solar and wind, is now judged to be better for the economy than nuclear. Internationally, an arc of change sweeps up through West Africa. Ghana will experience major changes in government and Algeria is also due for a change at the top.

The Full Moon on 25 September is in Aries in an opposition to Mercury and a square to Saturn. Uranus in the ninth house at London is trine Saturn. Economic growth remains steady. Organic agriculture booms as people return to traditional values. A leadership challenge in the Labour Party further weakens the party. India is recovering from a period of instability and presents a positive opportunity for smart investors. Denmark is in an assertive mood and anti-EU sentiments are strong. Canada develops a role as a major international broker and hosts a global peace conference.

In the *St. Leger* at Doncaster the winner may have been trained in the North. The Ayr *Gold Cup* may be won comfortably by a 6-year-old carrying 9st 1lb.

OCTOBER

For High Water add 5h 30m for Bristol, 4h 23m for Hull, 0h 43m for Leith; subtract 2h 21m for Dublin, 1h 26m for Greenock, 2h 29m for Liverpool.

D of M	D of W	Festivals, Events and Anniversaries	Sun at London Rises	Sun at London Sets	High Water at London Bridge am	High Water at London Bridge pm	Moon at London Rises	Moon at London Sets	Weather
			h m	h m	h m	h m	h m	h m	
1	M	Theresa May b. 1956	6:00	17:38	06 16	18 34	21:34	12:57	Summer returns! A colourful autumn bonus as fine weather reappears at intervals. Not until the close will the general pattern become more variable with ensuing damp westerly winds.
2	Tu	Marie Stopes d. 1958	6:02	17:36	06 59	19 26	22:31	13:59	
3	W	Aerosol patent 1941	6:04	17:33	07 53	20 33	23:39	14:53	
4	Th	Charlton Heston b. 1923	6:05	17:31	09 09	22 05	—	15:37	
5	F	Love Me Do released 1962	6:07	17:29	10 46	23 30	0:54	16:14	
6	Sa	Yom Kippur war beg. 1973	6:09	17:27	—	12 08	2:13	16:44	
7	Su	Battle of Lepanto 1571	6:10	17:24	00 44	13 11	3:33	17:11	
8	M	Baroness Boothroyd b. 1929	6:12	17:22	01 43	14 01	4:53	17:35	
9	Tu	Feast of St Denis	6:14	17:20	02 31	14 44	6:12	17:59	
10	W	Edith Piaf d. 1963	6:15	17:18	03 13	15 23	7:29	18:23	
11	Th	Children's Hour began 1926	6:17	17:16	03 52	16 01	8:44	18:50	
12	F	Brighton bombing 1984	6:19	17:13	04 28	16 04	9:56	19:19	
13	Sa	Queen longest reign 2016	6:20	17:11	05 03	17 17	11:03	19:54	
14	Su	Battle of Hastings 1066	6:22	17:09	05 37	17 55	12:05	20:35	
15	M	Great Storm 1987	6:24	17:07	06 10	18 34	12:59	21:22	
16	Tu	Skye Bridge open 1995	6:25	17:05	06 44	19 17	13:46	22:15	
17	W	Rita Hayworth b. 1918	6:27	17:03	07 25	20 14	14:25	23:13	
18	Th	Martina Navratilova b. 1956	6:29	17:01	08 23	21 36	14:58	—	
19	F	Diwali	6:31	16:59	09 58	22 55	15:26	0:15	
20	Sa	Sydney Opera Hs. op. 1973	6:32	16:56	11 21	—	15:50	1:20	
21	Su	Benjamin Netanyahu b. 1949	6:34	16:54	00 01	12 23	16:12	2:26	
22	M	Derek Jacobi b. 1938	6:36	16:52	00 56	13 11	16:33	3:34	
23	Tu	Pete Burns d. 2016	6:38	16:50	01 40	13 52	16:54	4:44	
24	W	United Nations Day	6:39	16:48	02 17	14 28	17:16	5:56	
25	Th	US invade Grenada 1983	6:41	16:46	02 52	15 03	17:41	7:09	
26	F	Yom Kippur war ends 1973	6:43	16:44	03 28	15 40	18:10	8:24	
27	Sa	John Cleese b. 1939	6:44	16:42	04 04	16 18	18:45	9:39	
28	Su	Erasmus b. 1466	6:46	16:41	04 41	16 57	19:30	10:51	
29	M	Suez Crisis begins 1956	6:48	16:39	05 19	17 38	20:24	11:56	
30	Tu	Aspirin on sale 1905	6:50	16:37	05 58	18 24	21:28	12:53	
31	W	Hallowe'en	6:52	16:35	06 43	19 19	22:41	13:39	

			Days	Hours	Mins
MOON'S	☾	Last Quarter	2	09	45
PHASES	●	New Moon	9	03	46
OCTOBER	☽	First Quarter	16	18	01
2018	○	Full Moon	24	16	45
	☾	Last Quarter	31	16	40

All times on this page are GMT (BST to 28 October + 1 hour)

PREDICTIONS

The New Moon on 9 October is in Libra in a square to Pluto and a quincunx to Neptune on the seventh cusp at London. The British government will suffer from financial muddle and attempts to balance the books are thrown off track by short-term decisions. Medical technology is moving very fast and GP surgeries will be offering remote consultations. Innovative communication technology could be using DNA and other biological matter in computing. Egypt plays an important diplomatic role in Middle East peace. Japan launches a diplomatic offensive to guarantee peace in the Far East.

The Full Moon on 24 October is in Taurus, rising at London, in a conjunction with Uranus, a trine with Saturn and an opposition with Venus. Public opinion is very volatile. Legal battles rise to the top of the agenda and the courts will intervene in foreign affairs. The situation is very complex and there may be multiple judgements which confuse the UK's attempts to build a new relationship with Europe. The security services should defeat a grade-one cyber attack on the UK and its allies. There will also be major developments in the roll-out of smart home technology, in which our domestic lives are connected to the web.

The winner at Newmarket's *Cesarewitch Heritage Handicap* may be a 4-year-old carrying 9st 1lb. Ascot's *Queen Elizabeth II Stakes* may be won by a 3-year-old carrying 8st 11lb.

NOVEMBER

For High Water add 5h 30m for Bristol, 4h 23m for Hull, 0h 43m for Leith; subtract 2h 21m for Dublin, 1h 26m for Greenock, 2h 29m for Liverpool.

D of M	D of W	Festivals, Events and Anniversaries	Sun at London Rises	Sun at London Sets	High Water at London Bridge am	High Water at London Bridge pm	Moon at London Rises	Moon at London Sets	Weather
			h m	h m	h m	h m	h m	h m	
1	Th	All Saints' Day	6:53	16:33	07 39	20 31	23:57	14:17	A short-lived rush of wind and rain at the start, especially in the North, quietens to bring night fogs. Variable temperatures and windy spells near the end with one or two storms.
2	F	Day of the Dead, Mexico	6:55	16:31	08 57	21 55	—	14:48	
3	Sa	Lulu b. 1948	6:57	16:30	10 28	23 12	1:16	15:14	
4	Su	UNESCO established 1946	6:59	16:28	11 44	—	2:34	15:38	
5	M	Bonfire Night	7:00	16:26	00 22	12 46	3:51	16:01	
6	Tu	Nigel Havers b. 1949	7:02	16:24	01 20	13 37	5:07	16:24	
7	W	Diwali	7:04	16:23	02 08	14 20	6:23	16:49	
8	Th	Berlin Wall breached 1989	7:06	16:21	02 49	14 59	7:36	17:17	
9	F	Dylan Thomas d. 1953	7:07	16:20	03 26	15 37	8:46	17:49	
10	Sa	Kristallnacht 1938	7:09	16:18	04 00	16 16	9:52	18:27	
11	Su	Remembrance Sunday	7:11	16:17	04 34	16 53	10:51	19:11	
12	M	1st London-B'ton rally 1927	7:13	16:15	05 07	17 30	11:41	20:02	
13	Tu	Battle of Alnwick 1093	7:14	16:14	05 38	18 07	12:24	20:59	
14	W	Prince of Wales b. 1948	7:16	16:12	06 11	18 46	12:59	22:00	
15	Th	Richmal Crompton b. 1890	7:18	16:11	06 48	19 33	13:29	23:04	
16	F	Clark Gable d. 1960	7:20	16:09	07 37	20 37	13:54	—	
17	Sa	Rock Hudson b. 1925	7:21	16:08	08 43	21 58	14:16	0:09	
18	Su	James Coburn d. 2002	7:23	16:07	10 20	23 05	14:37	1:16	
19	M	Dennis Taylor b. 1949	7:25	16:06	11 28	—	14:57	2:24	
20	Tu	Pr. Elizabeth m. Philip 1947	7:26	16:04	00 02	12 23	15:18	3:34	
21	W	World Television Day	7:28	16:03	00 53	13 10	15:41	4:47	
22	Th	Thanksgiving (USA)	7:29	16:02	01 38	13 53	16:08	6:03	
23	F	Andrew Sachs d. 2016	7:31	16:01	02 21	14 36	16:41	7:19	
24	Sa	*Black Beauty* pub. 1879	7:33	16:00	03 03	15 19	17:23	7:35	
25	Su	Fidel Castro d. 2016	7:34	15:59	03 45	16 03	18:15	9:46	
26	M	Tina Turner b. 1939	7:36	15:58	04 27	16 47	19:17	10:48	
27	Tu	William Blake b. 1757	7:37	15:57	05 09	17 33	20:29	11:40	
28	W	Enid Blyton d. 1968	7:39	15:57	05 51	18 23	21:46	12:21	
29	Th	Louisa M. Alcott b. 1832	7:40	15:56	06 38	19 20	23:04	12:53	
30	F	St Andrew's Day	7:42	15:55	07 34	20 27	—	13:21	

MOON'S PHASES NOVEMBER 2018		Days	Hours	Mins
●	New Moon	7	16	01
☽	First Quarter	15	14	54
○	Full Moon	23	05	39
☾	Last Quarter	30	00	18

All times on this page are GMT

PREDICTIONS

The New Moon on 7 November falls in Scorpio in the seventh house at London, in a trine with Neptune. Pluto is on the Midheaven at London. Long-lost scandals will resurface and there will be prosecutions for crimes committed many years ago. The government could be rocked by a major ministerial resignation. New security measures should be put in place at Westminster to protect politicians and staff. There could also be problems on the London tube network. The gun lobby in the USA drives through further rights for gun owners. In Europe the key area of change is the Balkans, and long lost passions cause instability in Bosnia, Serbia and Macedonia.

The Full Moon on the 23 November falls in Gemini in the seventh house at London in a square to Mars and an opposition to Jupiter. Venus is opposed to Uranus. Free choice is the order of the day. This is a moment of maximum tension which is very difficult for emotional relationships. Allies will fall out with each other. Enemies will go to war over matters of principle. Religious militants will be on the rise. Venezuela's government may finally fall, after a steep economic collapse. France is establishing a new role on the world stage, intervening militarily.

In the Newbury *Hennessy Gold Cup Chase* (which could run in early December), a 5-year-old carrying 9st 6lb may prove the winner.

DECEMBER

For High Water add 5h 30m for Bristol, 4h 23m for Hull, 0h 43m for Leith; subtract 2h 21m for Dublin, 1h 26m for Greenock, 2h 29m for Liverpool.

D of M	D of W	Festivals, Events and Anniversaries	Sun at London Rises	Sun at London Sets	High Water at London Bridge am	High Water at London Bridge pm	Moon at London Rises	Moon at London Sets	Wea-ther
			h m	h m	h m	h m	h m	h m	
1	Sa	World AIDS Day	7:43	15:55	08 46	21 37	0:22	13:45	Cold, frosty, foggy nights until, after mid-month, milder and sunny weather intervenes. This continues until Christmas when northerly winds and a cold, unsettled pattern ensues.
2	Su	Advent	7:45	15:54	10 04	22 46	1:38	14:07	
3	M	First heart transplant 1967	7:46	15:53	11 14	23 54	2:53	14:29	
4	Tu	Ronnie Corbett b. 1930	7:47	15:53	—	12 17	4:07	14:52	
5	W	Oscar Niemeyer d. 2012	7:48	15:52	00 54	13 12	5:20	15:18	
6	Th	Feast of St Nicholas	7:50	15:52	01 44	13 59	6:31	15:47	
7	F	Armenian earthquake 1988	7:51	15:52	02 27	14 41	7:38	16:22	
8	Sa	John Lennon murdered 1980	7:52	15:51	03 05	15 20	8:40	17:04	
9	Su	*Coronation Street* bgns 1960	7:53	15:51	03 39	15 59	9:35	17:52	
10	M	Pneumatic tyre patent 1845	7:54	15:51	04 12	16 36	10:21	18:47	
11	Tu	Willie Rushton d. 1996	7:55	15:51	04 44	17 12	10:59	19:46	
12	W	Robert Browning d. 1889	7:56	15:51	05 17	17 47	11:31	20:49	
13	Th	Dick Van Dyke b. 1925	7:57	15:51	05 50	18 24	11:58	21:53	
14	F	Jane Birkin b. 1946	7:58	15:51	06 26	19 05	12:21	22:59	
15	Sa	Piccadilly line opened 1906	7:59	15:51	07 07	19 52	12:41	—	
16	Su	Pilgrim Fathers landed 1620	8:00	15:51	07 56	20 52	13:01	0:05	
17	M	Dominic Lawson b. 1956	8:01	15:51	08 59	22 03	13:21	1:13	
18	Tu	Zsa Zsa Gabor d. 2016	8:01	15:52	10 23	23 07	13:42	2:23	
19	W	*Rimet* trophy stolen 1983	8:02	15:52	11 32	—	13:07	3:36	
20	Th	John Steinbeck d. 1968	8:03	15:52	00 07	12 30	13:36	4:52	
21	F	Winter solstice (22 23)	8:03	15:53	01 03	13 23	15:13	6:09	
22	Sa	Peggy Ashcroft b. 1907	8:04	15:53	01 55	14 14	16:00	7:24	
23	Su	BBC radio news b'ns 1922	8:04	15:54	02 44	15 04	16:59	8:33	
24	M	Christmas Eve	8:05	15:55	03 31	15 53	18:09	9:31	
25	Tu	Christmas Day	8:05	15:55	04 17	16 41	19:28	10:19	
26	W	Boxing Day/St Stephen	8:05	15:56	05 02	17 30	20:48	10:56	
27	Th	Carrie Fisher d. 2016	8:05	15:57	05 47	18 19	22:09	11:26	
28	F	Debbie Reynolds d. 2016	8:06	15:58	06 33	19 12	23:27	11:51	
29	Sa	William Gladstone b. 1809	8:06	15:58	07 23	20 09	—	12:14	
30	Su	Tiger Woods b. 1975	8:06	15:59	08 23	21 10	0:43	12:36	
31	M	New Year's Eve/Hogmanay	8:06	16:00	09 31	22 12	1:57	12:58	

MOON'S PHASES DECEMBER 2018			Days	Hours	Mins
●	New Moon		7	07	20
☽	First Quarter		15	11	49
○	Full Moon		22	17	48
☾	Last Quarter		29	09	34

All times on this page are GMT

PREDICTIONS

The New Moon on 7 December is in Sagittarius in the first house at London, in a square to Mars and Neptune. The mood of the times is optimistic, inspirational and adventurous, but also reckless. Levels of corruption and fraud remain high. There is a high chance of the world drifting into war through muddle rather than intention. Missiles may be launched accidentally. There will be major advances in space technology with new forms of engine propelling rockets further than thought possible over the coming years. Scientists will trigger excitement with announcements of significant discoveries about new mineral life in the deep oceans.

The Full Moon on 22 December falls in Cancer in the twelfth house at London. The international situation looks more relaxed and conflicts will be resolved by shuttle diplomacy and high-level meetings. Oil spills from pipelines or tankers are possible in the Canadian Midwest and Great Lakes area, and the Great Barrier Reef. The USA attempts to expand its legal jurisdiction to other countries and arrests foreign citizens. The drug wars in Mexico hit a new height with the army called in to patrol areas of major cities, and martial law likely for several states. We can expect a new government in Romania.

The *Welsh National* at Chepstow may see a 6-year-old carrying 11st 3lb first past the winning post, whilst Kempton's *King George VI* chase may favour a 7-year-old.

49

Claudia Winkleman

© PA Images

TV presenter, radio broadcaster and journalist Claudia Winkleman was born on 15 January 1972. Claudia has no less than three planets in the earthy sign of Capricorn. This gives her good stamina, persistence and patience but it also means for certain that there is a large part of her personality that only family and close friends ever really know. What you see is not necessarily what you truly get with this often apparently zany personality, as a deeper emotional side lies hidden beneath the bubbly exterior. With Venus in quirky Aquarius and Jupiter at home in its own sign of Sagittarius, it is true that Claudia possesses a great sense of fun and rarely takes herself too seriously. In terms of planetary spread, Claudia's chart is mostly placed between Libra and Pisces, which gives her deep and penetrative insight, and an intuition that is unlikely to let her down.

From an early start on radio and around the fringes of television Claudia Winkleman's career grew steadily. Like the true Capricorn she is, she avoided pushing too hard but never slackened the effort to 'get on'. Ultimately she now finds herself at the very centre of the BBC's Saturday and Sunday blockbuster *Strictly Come Dancing*. Claudia is eminently suited to this role and it will serve her well but there are more places to go and a great deal more to achieve for the steady but relentless mover she cannot avoid being. Expect some 'serious' television to be part of her future remit, together with more journalism, as well as the possibility of a series of children's books.

Claudia has Venus in Aquarius. Whilst all the Capricorn in her chart keeps her grounded, her Venus feeds a desire to shock on occasions and fuels a great sense of the absurd. The 'under the fringe stare' for which she is so famous suits Claudia well because very little escapes her gaze. Under the fun she is fiercely humanitarian, a physical and spiritual traveller, a deep thinker and a person who has much more savvy than aspects of her public persona would tend to suggest.

Claudia will almost certainly host her own chat show in the not too distant future and will probably continue to be a television and film critic, but Old Moore predicts that the world of literature has a great deal to offer before the next few years are out. On the way through what are likely to be a few busy years ahead it is to be hoped Claudia ensures that she takes time to rest because even tough Capricorn is not indestructible. Claudia almost certainly has a 'family first' motto and this, together with time spent with those closest to her, should stand her in good stead for what lies ahead.

LIBRA BORN PEOPLE
Birthdays: 24 September to 23 October inclusive
Planet: Venus. Birthstone: Opal. Lucky day: Friday

Keynote for the Year: *You may have your work cut out with responsibilities at home this year, but trends affecting finances look especially promising. Get planning, Libra!*

JANUARY: MAIN TRENDS: 11–12 If you eliminate old situations and focus on renewal you can transform your life. **18–19** Listening to a partner's opinion may prove useful in the short term – keep abreast of what's going on in the world. **20–21** There should be plenty going on domestically to make you feel rewarded – a good period for attending to minor improvements at home. **KEY DATES: HIGHS 8–9** Visualise what you want to achieve, put the plan into action and give it everything. **LOWS 22–24** Proceed carefully and avoid all risks. If you are not working over these days things will be easier for you.

FEBRUARY: MAIN TRENDS: 10–11 This is a great period for one-to-one relationships, when you can bring out the best in everyone and boost your own popularity. **18–19** Capitalise on your ability to win people's confidence by liaising closely with colleagues. **21–22** Relationships are rewarding wherever you happen to be, and there may be new faces on the horizon. **KEY DATES: HIGHS 4–5** The wheels of progress move smoothly – just for you! **LOWS 19–20** Not a good time to rush into something with all guns blazing. Get some rest instead.

MARCH: MAIN TRENDS: 6–7 Security is the key issue now, and you may find it is possible to sort out some financial matters for the better. **16–17** Several avenues of communication may open up to you now, and you won't be happy to be confined to just one. **20–21** You may be able to make the best of new opportunities career wise – a rethink may now lead to further success. **KEY DATES: HIGHS 3–5; 31** You should find individual and professional aims to be easily attainable and that it is possible to get your own way. **LOWS 18–19** Low energy levels are never an excuse for not doing your best, although you should still keep your targets realistic.

APRIL: MAIN TRENDS: 2–3 Throw yourself into work and be as industrious as possible and you should reap rewards. A positive trend for health, too. **20–21** Curious and chatty, this is a great period for casual conversations with friends and loved ones. **24–25** Friends and partners should now prove invaluable to whatever you are doing in life. **KEY DATES: HIGHS 1; 27–28** Now is the time to pursue your heart's desire – assert yourself positively and new ventures will almost certainly prove successful. **LOWS 14–15** Let go of high expectations and work happily within those constraints.

MAY: MAIN TRENDS: 14–15 Put to good use current trends favouring good communication and an analytic mind and try a little problem solving. **19–20** Today you may be bored with routine so put yourself at the forefront of the action and be versatile. **21–22** Don't rely on luck or believe everything you hear today as this is a potentially deceptive influence where you should beware of false optimism. **KEY DATES: HIGHS 24–26** Look out for a small success at work, especially if you push your luck just a little. **LOWS 12–13** A low-key mood prevails at this time, especially relating to partnerships.

JUNE: MAIN TRENDS: 13–14 Your practical affairs may undergo minor change as you use good judgement to re-evaluate your goals and plan ahead for the short term. **23–24** You may be able to broaden your contacts at work as your superiors may become increasingly approachable. **29–30** Travel and social trends look good at this time and some friendly support may help you to widen your horizons and enlarge your world. **KEY DATES: HIGHS 21–22** Make this a period of initiative and self-reliance as trends suggest that personal enterprises are the most successful. **LOWS 8–9** Under a heavy workload and with tasks mounting up your energy and productivity can be easily depleted – delegate wherever possible.

JULY: MAIN TRENDS: 1–2 Hard work pays off and new plans may lead to progress now, whether socially or practically. **10–11** There may be plenty of opportunities to dominate the spotlight now, and if you are seeking romance you may get more than bargained for! **22–23** Take advantage of this helpful trend by keeping eyes and ears open for new information related to current plans and programmes. **KEY DATES: HIGHS 18–19** A new project could fire you with vigour, so aim a little higher than usual in your objectives, Libra. **LOWS 5–7** Fortune is not on your side so there may be minor setbacks. Pace yourself accordingly.

AUGUST: MAIN TRENDS: 6–7 You find fulfillment being part of a team or being surrounded by like-minded friends. **13–14** Under this influence you should think about travel, seeking out new horizons or getting in touch with a long-distance associate. **23–24** Socially you have the capacity to attract the right kind of attention. An excellent time for visiting places of entertainment and fun. **KEY DATES: HIGHS 14–15** Matters at work should be smooth sailing now as superiors and colleagues lend you their help. **LOWS 1–3; 29–30** Prepare for some minor setbacks, as fortune is not on your side. Try to relax and ride out the trend.

SEPTEMBER: MAIN TRENDS: 6–7 Intimate talks and discussions should be fruitful now as you have an instinctive talent for saying just the right thing. **9–10** Appointments and meetings are well highlighted in your chart so use your communicative talents to sway the opinions of those around you. **23–24** You know how to get the best out of others and this trend may see you widening your social circle as you express yourself. **KEY DATES: HIGHS 11–12** Whether in ongoing projects or getting new things off of the ground, this is your monthly highpoint. **LOWS 25–26** Daily life could be unstable and prone to sudden changes of fortune. Try to keep things on an even keel.

OCTOBER: MAIN TRENDS: 10–11 Under this trend you should be winning through in social and romantic activities. Take the lead and let others enjoy your company! **25–26** Your intellectual powers are at their best and your decisions show superior judgement. Others can't touch you in important debate. **30–31** A promising time in which you should reach out to new vistas to find fulfilling experiences. Long journeys are particularly favoured. **KEY DATES: HIGHS 8–9** With nothing to stand in the way of your path to progress, don't be afraid to take decisions. **LOWS 22–24** Beware of hasty actions based on emotional impulses. Indulge yourself a little.

NOVEMBER: MAIN TRENDS: 11–12 Romantic trends are certainly on the up and social matters ought to keep you happy, too. **15–16** The planets make this a good day to make new friends and also favour personal relationships and affairs of the heart. **22–23** You would benefit from some peace and quiet away from the hustle and bustle, and the family scene looks to be the best way of achieving this. **KEY DATES: HIGHS 4–5** In a determined mood, this is a good time to improve efficiency or test your luck. **LOWS 19–20** Avoid defeatism and a negative frame of mind – if you are overambitious now, life will show you just where to give up!

DECEMBER: MAIN TRENDS: 4–5 Under favourable trends for finances, this could be a day of considerable profit if you play your cards right. **12–13** Even if you are very busy at work, don't let this mean that you miss too much of what's going on, news-wise, in the outer world. **21–22** The home is the best place to be – outdoor life seems to have little appeal right now. Focus on family issues. **KEY DATES: HIGHS 2–3; 29–30** A mental peak when your judgement and timing is good. You may enjoy a real sense of achievement. **LOWS 16–17** Your energy is running low so hang back with crucial decisions and keep your demands of others simple as well.

SCORPIO BORN PEOPLE
Birthdays: 24 October to 22 November inclusive
Planets: Mars, Pluto. Birthstone: Topaz. Lucky day: Tuesday

Keynote for the Year: *You can really turn things to your advantage this year with lucky Jupiter in your sign, whether that's in personal or professional developments.*

JANUARY: MAIN TRENDS: 12–13 Everyday life may become a little less secure due to certain changes; don't be afraid of this but view it as a spring clean. **18–19** The usual chat now brings a feelgood factor which should lead to pleasurable encounters as well as useful information. **20–21** Trends may provide you with some influence in important financial negotiations, certainly you should not now settle for second best. **KEY DATES: HIGHS 10–11** Lady Luck may lend you an unexpected helping hand! **LOWS 25–26** During this planetary low you may lack the energy to deal with even everyday matters – admitting and accepting this is the best course of action.

FEBRUARY: MAIN TRENDS: 10–11 Trends indicate that you will be taking a new approach so perhaps use this influence to look for new solutions to old problems. **18–19** The path ahead to professional success may become more obvious and you should be able to show superiors what you're made of. **23–24** Your capable thinking could prove very useful now if you focus on practical issues and developing them. **KEY DATES: HIGHS 6–8** Allow yourself to become immersed in new plans for the future and go for them! **LOWS 21–22** Take care to resist the manipulative or coercive tactics of others.

MARCH: MAIN TRENDS: 8–9 Trends give you the ability to attract others with the power of your charm, making this a great time for romance or social gatherings. **17–18** Risks don't frighten you and you have plenty of energy so go for what you want, but keep a sensible approach. **22–23** Under favourable trends for communications, discussions and negotiations may turn out far better than expected. **KEY DATES: HIGHS 6–7** This is a great time to begin something new – the more ambitious the better. **LOWS 20–21** You may experience some challenging changes to routines. Don't wear yourself out over trivialities.

APRIL: MAIN TRENDS: 4–5 With plenty to keep you alert, interested and, above all, busy this is the time to apply yourself. **20–21** Spring-clean time both physically and mentally. Clear out whatever has outlived its usefulness in your life, whether a material object or a situation. **24–25** Friendships keep you smiling and they may now have an educational quality – prepare to have your eyes opened! **KEY DATES: HIGHS 2–3; 29–30** Your best time of the month: a phase of solid advancement, growth and optimism. **LOWS 16–18** Ease off major activities to save yourself time and energy as they are not likely to proceed smoothly now.

MAY: MAIN TRENDS: 12–13 You may feel frustrated by your lack of influence in certain situations; in fact, you may have to seek out special help from someone today. **19–20** Get out into the wide, blue yonder for a mentally uplifting experience. The further your travels take you the better. **21–22** Matters taking place in groups, especially socially, are positively highlighted in your chart and there's strength in numbers now. **KEY DATES: HIGHS 27–28** There should be nothing to prevent you finally turning a corner with your plans now. **LOWS 14–15** Step back to assess the effect you are having on others and you may find you are not getting through to them.

JUNE: MAIN TRENDS: 13–14 You can benefit from communicating and discussing ideas with other people. You are at your best when this two-way process is happening. **21–22** Your laid back and charming manner may prove attractive to others and you work best at the centre of a lot of activity and teamwork. **29–30** With the energy you now have you can afford a confident attitude to overcoming obstacles in your path – go for it! **KEY DATES: HIGHS 23–24** One of your best days of the month for beginning new projects or getting others on side. **LOWS 10–11** Don't now take on any major or time-consuming tasks as your energy levels may be lower than usual.

JULY: MAIN TRENDS: 1–2 This trend may put you in the picture regarding current short term aims, and it looks as though information received could now prove unexpectedly useful. **10–11** A positive time for friendships when you may meet new people and benefit from contact with others generally. **22–23** You could have some promising ideas at work. A good time to bring a major plan to completion and give it the finishing touch. **KEY DATES: HIGHS 20–21** Your strength lies in your ability to bring friends and colleagues around to your way of thinking. **LOWS 8–9** A good time to slow things down as your spirits and vitality may be on the wane.

AUGUST: MAIN TRENDS: 6–7 Your personal charisma and sunny disposition help you to make an impact on others. Social and romantic relationships tend to be harmonious. **13–14** Meeting other people keeps you stimulated, and you probably have a talent for inspiring, even teaching, others now. **23–24** A well-disposed highlight on work must mean major things are happening but don't allow the excitement to lead you to lose sight of the finer details. **KEY DATES: HIGHS 16–18** Begin a new project or speed ahead with existing ones. **LOWS 4–5; 31** Confusion reigns as even the best-laid schemes may fail. Put them on the back burner for now.

SEPTEMBER: MAIN TRENDS: 6–7 Perhaps you don't want to waste energy on anything demanding or tedious but take care not to leave anything half finished at work. **9–10** Communications are highlighted and you will be sensitive to the feelings of others today. Gain some insight by listening to your inner voice. **23–24** Make the best of your social life as you get on well with others and make an impact. **KEY DATES: HIGHS 13–14** Your prospects look good at work as your relationships with superiors are good. **LOWS 1; 27–29** Don't overface yourself with obligations and duties today that you could wind down if you chose to.

OCTOBER: MAIN TRENDS: 12–13 Financially you may be on a winning streak and there is planetary assistance as you try to consolidate. **23–24** Your best moments come through work and there may be more than one way to make progress. **30–31** A time of relative stability and security when financial matters are either on the up or can be firmed up. **KEY DATES: HIGHS 10–11** You ought now to feel confident and self-assured and can motivate others just as easily as yourself. **LOWS 25–26** Don't allow domestic issues to affect the way you work, especially as you find it hard to focus now.

NOVEMBER: MAIN TRENDS: 11–12 Your love life looks to be smooth and sweet as your powers of attraction increase. **15–16** Now you should have abundant energy for personal activities. Remember 'variety is the spice of life' should be the prevailing motto. **23–24** Capitalise on your natural talent for communication. The need to maintain connections with others is a big motivation for you and pays dividends. **KEY DATES: HIGHS 7–8** A potentially lucky period – be prepared to act quickly in some situations. **LOWS 21–22** This trend makes you susceptible to misunderstandings, especially if there may be conflicts about a project's direction. Think things through before you act.

DECEMBER: MAIN TRENDS: 2–3 A regenerative phase when certain issues may come to an end; whatever is not working out in your life requires attention. **12–13** This influence may see you moving your life more constructively in business and relationships – you have the means to change for the better. **21–22** Expect to be in an optimistic frame of mind and keen to expand your horizons. **KEY DATES: HIGHS 4–5; 31** There's much you can do to aid the cause of progress during another phase when your luck may be in. **LOWS 18–20** Highly sensitive to others now, you may become overwhelmed by duties. Careful, Scorpio!

SAGITTARIUS BORN PEOPLE
Birthdays: 23 November to 21 December inclusive
Planet: Jupiter. Birthstone: Turquoise. Lucky day: Thursday

Keynote for the Year: *Financially, you should budget wisely, but the work you put in at the start of the year will pay off later. A matter from the past may be revealing.*

JANUARY: MAIN TRENDS: 10–11 Trends influence the personal aspects of life; be as open as possible with loved ones about your feelings. **18–19** You may receive some unexpected good luck at work, and with the help of your co-workers or boss a project may get off the ground. **20–21** Present trends keep you involved socially and you shine in teamwork in large groups. **KEY DATES: HIGHS 12–14** Decisions made now could turn out better than you might have expected. **LOWS 27–28** Expect to feel tired at the moment. This is also a particularly bad time for unwise spending, investment or financial speculation.

FEBRUARY: MAIN TRENDS: 11–12 This is not a time of extroversion, nor the best time to start any great projects. Consolidate what you have and pull back a bit. **18–19** Unexpected pressures may arise at home now and you may have to drop everything else you were doing. Professionally this may lead to a small setback. **20–21** In terms of your career prospects it's not so much what you know, but *who* you know that makes the difference! **KEY DATES: HIGHS 9–10** A time for getting ahead with a bit of positive thinking and planning. **LOWS 23–24** A good time to finish up any unresolved business – the longer you wait, the worse it may get.

MARCH: MAIN TRENDS: 6–7 Enjoy some leisure, especially in creative pursuits. A romance also looks very promising now. **17–18** Under a tricky trend for communication you may be left in the dark over the outcome of a personal decision, or find yourself at cross-purposes with someone. **20–21** Now you will enjoy the limelight socially, hiding your light under a bushel is simply not for you. **KEY DATES: HIGHS 8–9** You're not about to miss a trick when it comes to what Lady Luck has in store, and your perception helps you beat the competition. **LOWS 22–23** You may stumble over some obstacles just now so try to take things easily.

APRIL: MAIN TRENDS: 1–2 Let your personality shine during this natural energy boost and time of accomplishment. **21–22** All family relationships should be rewarding and loved ones at home really bring out the best in you. A pleasantly nostalgic influence. **24–25** Good financial trends may help you to obtain the good things of life more easily than usual. You can make this a time of both consolidation and gains. **KEY DATES: HIGHS 4–5** Be prepared for any chance to achieve your goals and take them when they come along. **LOWS 19–20** Don't expect to make massive headway socially as you may prefer your own company.

MAY: MAIN TRENDS: 13–15 Devote yourself to any important task that comes along; being 'in the know' professionally could make a big difference to your life. **19–20** You may quickly become bored with routine and feel the need to explore, entertain original ideas and broaden your horizons. **21–22** A warm, intimate and co-operative atmosphere at home should enable you to get closer to someone. **KEY DATES: HIGHS 2–3; 29–30** You may find yourself in a prominent position and you can accomplish things which will amaze others. **LOWS 16–17** Figures in authority may be more demanding than usual, requiring you to work harder – don't overdo it!

JUNE MAIN TRENDS: 14–15 Career wise you can now go forth with a number of good cards in your hand and some unexpected help may also be available. **21–22** Domestic issues are positively highlighted, especially those related to the past. **29–30** Don't be tempted to participate in unrealistic, unworkable plans. It may be wise to keep your eyes open and watch out for pitfalls right now.

KEY DATES: HIGHS 26–27 A busy phase of events may lie ahead and this can be a time of interesting, productive change. **LOWS 12–13** You may have to err on the side of caution with decisions. Perhaps let a trusted partner make them for you.

JULY: MAIN TRENDS: 1–2 Capitalise on the opportunity to do something different or to get some variety into your life; multi-tasking at work should be no problem. **12–13** Plenty of subtlety may be required to understand others, now. If you can overturn certain trying situations and put them in the past, do so. **25–26** Broaden your horizons and take any opportunity to get away from it all. A great time to be outdoors, especially with new friends. **KEY DATES: HIGHS 22–24** Another good day for progress, perhaps bringing you the opportunity to make creative changes. **LOWS 10–11** You may have your work cut out keeping life on an even keel so proceed slowly.

AUGUST: MAIN TRENDS: 8–9 A power struggle could be in the offing as a person or event challenges your peace of mind and certain changes are required. **13–14** Family and domestic matters could be extra rewarding – enjoy the quieter side of life and suspend practical initiatives. **23–24** The spotlight falls on short-term plans and financial schemes; someone may provide information to help you get a clearer sense of direction. **KEY DATES: HIGHS 19–20** A word in the right ear could work wonders and lead to a lucky break! **LOWS 6–7** Accept that life may feel uneventful and your enthusiasm is lacking and take things easily.

SEPTEMBER: MAIN TRENDS: 6–7 Being in the middle of the social and romantic action really suits you now but bear in mind you may need to compromise if your ideas don't tally with someone else's. **9–10** During a slack time for professional progress, your thoughts turn to the good old days and you should be quite content with that. **23–24** With patience you can achieve bigger and better constructive changes at work, but avoid the temptation to be a know-it-all! **KEY DATES: HIGHS 15–16** Keep a sharp eye out for opportunities of all kinds. **LOWS 2–4; 30** A quieter period when you should take a back seat away from the action.

OCTOBER: MAIN TRENDS: 10–11 Under some generally very positive trends, focus on your creative abilities and living the good life. Expect to also have a powerful impact on others socially. **23–24** If you have an opportunity to influence others, make sure you use it in the most appropriate way. **30–31** It becomes easier to make good decisions about long-range plans so put some time aside to consider these. **KEY DATES: HIGHS 12–14** Act upon the urge to get things done as quickly as possible and you could reap the rewards. **LOWS 1; 27–28** Don't take any risks with your time and energy today or these precious commodities could be wasted.

NOVEMBER: MAIN TRENDS: 11–12 The stars place a beneficial accent on joint monetary matters. Close relationships may now have much to do with improving your finances. **15–16** Your ego knows no bounds and will get you noticed everywhere, but you fare best in romantic and recreational activities. **21–22** Your likeability is probably at a premium helping you to get the best out of others, especially in group-based encounters. **KEY DATES: HIGHS 9–10** A physical peak where you seem to be on top form and it's easier to accomplish your aims. **LOWS 23–24** Pace yourself now and accept the occasional small blip in your progress.

DECEMBER: MAIN TRENDS: 2–3 Show off your best side and express your ideas and people will understand you. Career interests are positively highlighted. **12–13** Things work best in partnerships for you now and get-togethers with others prove highly rewarding as you please and impress people. **23–24** Others may find you exciting and original to be around as you are open to new ideas. A long trip could be rewarding. **KEY DATES: HIGHS 6–7** Use your talent for self-promotion if stimulating new ideas and opportunities come your way. **LOWS 21–22** Possibly a run-of-the-mill type of period but this will only be a temporary phase.

CAPRICORN BORN PEOPLE
Birthdays: 22 December to 20 January inclusive
Planet: Saturn. Birthstone: Garnet. Lucky day: Saturday

Keynote for the Year: *Saturn, your sombre ruler, is in your sign now, encouraging hard work to achieve excellence. A good year for widening your social circles, too.*

JANUARY: MAIN TRENDS: 11–12 There may be good things happening in your career at this time – seize any initiative that could lead to advancement. **18–19** Now is the time to step out into the world and it may be an advantage to talk through your plans with a superior at work. **20–21** Things in the family work best for you during this period of nostalgia and contentment around the hearth and home. **KEY DATES: HIGHS 15–16** Something may step into your path and guide you in a new direction – consider this a lucky break. **LOWS 1–2; 29–30** A quiet period – don't take big risks, avoid unwarranted assumptions and take it easy.

FEBRUARY: MAIN TRENDS: 9–10 With support and encouragement you can reach higher goals in life, especially in your career. **18–19** Social get-togethers could be beneficial; take advantage of some quality time with friends and associates. **20–21** Don't believe everything you hear today: you may be tempted down certain paths that could eventually prove to have been deceptive. **KEY DATES: HIGHS 11–13** A positive moment when something or someone may allow you to realise your ambitions. **LOWS 25–26** A planetary lull patch when you may feel less enthusiastic than usual – be patient with yourself.

MARCH: MAIN TRENDS: 6–7 Your social life is top priority for you now and you may not be much use at work – you might even describe your feeling as rather lazy! **17–18** Follow your heart and give in to the urge to break away from routine and try different things. Get out and about if you can. **20–21** A new decisiveness takes hold of you as with only a little effort you take the initiative and expect the best. **KEY DATES: HIGHS 10–13** You can make a powerful impact during this period of high energy and physical activity. **LOWS 24–25** During this sluggish period overconfidence in dealing with setbacks could rebound on you – beware!

APRIL: MAIN TRENDS: 1–2 You may find it hard to adopt any kind of leading role and your strengths seem to be in advisory capacities and activities behind the scenes. **24–25** Your organisational ability is at its peak right now and your thinking is positive – this should garner great results. **26–27** You know how to be liked by others so use your instincts to take the initiative in social or romantic situations. **KEY DATES: HIGHS 7–8** Trends favour taking a calculated risk as just about anything is possible now. **LOWS 21–22** Not the best time to be overconfident, or to expect too much if you feel out of sorts. Ride out the trend.

MAY: MAIN TRENDS: 13–15 Although you are quick-witted, certain egocentric tendencies are at work which could provoke a flashpoint. At least you can get things done with sheer willpower. **16–17** Be alert when it comes to communication and business and don't sit around and wait – act. **21–22** Keep eyes and ears open for useful information especially if you become involved in interesting discussions. **KEY DATES: HIGHS 4–5; 31** Your powers of influence do seem to be at their height as others provide support and encouragement. **LOWS 18–19** If you experience some dispiriting delays to your plans, take time to recharge your batteries.

JUNE: MAIN TRENDS: 13–14 An appropriate time to make monetary decisions – you could be in a position to restructure finances and put things on a more secure footing. **21–22** The accent is on romance and fun and social life. You have a talent for creating an atmosphere of peace and harmony. **29–30** A favourable time to be working behind the scenes on plans and projects to be unveiled at a later date. **KEY DATES: HIGHS 1–2; 28–29** Don't allow doubters to put you off acting on any good ideas right now. **LOWS 14–15** Be aware that not everything you hear may be reliable under current trends, and there could be some misinformation floating about.

JULY: MAIN TRENDS: 1–2 Your self-confidence makes this a good time to express yourself and helps you to communicate your ideas. **10–11** There is a positive emphasis on your economic situation and monetary goals may now see some concrete results. **22–23** A great time to get things accomplished – especially professionally – and it should be easy for you to push forward. **KEY DATES: HIGHS 25–26** You should receive planetary support if you choose to make this an extremely dynamic time career wise. **LOWS 12–13** Even though your energy may be limited, that doesn't mean you can't enjoy self indulgences of just about any kind.

AUGUST: MAIN TRENDS: 6–7 Your outlook is positive and your belief in what you can achieve is greater than ever – so something good should happen! **13–14** At work, trends favour greater effectiveness and productivity, meaning that success should effortlessly follow. **24–25** You may have a talent for helping people and existing relationships are highly favoured; you may also have fruitful dealings with figures in authority. **KEY DATES: HIGHS 21–23** You have some natural advantages over others and this is the time to put them to the test. **LOWS 8–9** A so-so period should give you no cause to think that things are going wrong, but avoid high-risk situations.

SEPTEMBER: MAIN TRENDS: 7–8 Good things can come through your social life and personal relationships, and this should put you in the best of moods. **9–10** Now you can really make things happen – the force of your personality is strong and this is a great period for new beginnings. **23–24** Your personal influence over everyday matters may be less than you'd expected. Then again, you may find that you share emotions and insights with a trusted confidante. **KEY DATES: HIGHS 17–19** Decisiveness wins the day where major projects are concerned, especially if someone notes your positive attitude. **LOWS 5–6** If things go wrong, take stock of your affairs and rethink how you could have changed things for the better.

OCTOBER: MAIN TRENDS: 10–11 You may feel on top form right now and this is a fairly good time to effect changes in your personal life. **23–24** Day-to-day life may become more hectic – but try to complete everything on your agenda. Prioritise and keep distractions to a minimum. **27–28** Make whatever changes are needed in personal affairs and don't be afraid to mix business with pleasure. **KEY DATES: HIGHS 15–16** A propitious time for dreams and schemes – partners conspire to make life pleasurable. **LOWS 2–3; 29–30** Trends suggest that you may need to make sense out of a chaotic situation, but that you will be equal to the task.

NOVEMBER: MAIN TRENDS: 14–15 Take positive action to help you promote your own interests. Optimistic and in good cheer, everyone should be on your side. **15–16** Trends indicate time for a personal spring-clean – clear out the dead wood from your life and prepare the ground for new growth. **22–23** Reach out socially and geographically, in order to broaden your mental and physical horizons. **KEY DATES: HIGHS 11–13** A great time to try out a new, tempting idea, personally or career wise. **LOWS 25–26** Don't be hard on yourself if you can't seem to get your message across to someone – get an early night instead.

DECEMBER: MAIN TRENDS: 2–3 A positive period in which life seems to flow effortlessly and you can easily get where you want to be. **12–13** Think seriously about what you want from life and assess what is useful for you right now and what is not. **21–22** Increased responsibility could leave you feeling overburdened and compromise may be needed in relationships to preserve the status quo. **KEY DATES: HIGHS 9–10** New beginnings and fresh projects are positively highlighted around now. An energetic time when you may be able to get a lot done. **LOWS 23–24** Proceed cautiously with certain plans that go instinctively against the grain.

AQUARIUS BORN PEOPLE
Birthdays: 21 January to 19 February inclusive
Planets: Saturn, Uranus. Birthstone: Amethyst. Lucky day: Saturday

Keynote for the Year: *While you may have to confront your past, your career receives a boost this year. Look for new opportunities and the chance to expand your professional interests.*

JANUARY: MAIN TRENDS: 11–12 You may be happiest working alone now – a low-profile task might seem to suit you best, one where you can be your own boss. **15–16** This trend may bring an unexpected boost to your profession or finances, and this is certainly looks like a rosy time for most monetary dealings. **20–21** Your career continues to benefit from positive trends enabling you to accomplish a great deal more than usual. **KEY DATES: HIGHS 17–19** With high levels of physical energy you can now get ahead faster. **LOWS 3–4; 31** Not your most fortunate time so it would be wise to keep your expectations simple.

FEBRUARY: MAIN TRENDS: 10–11 A good time to consider positive change in your life or to ask someone for a favour. **18–19** Make this an adventurous period and take every opportunity to do something new and exciting, so long as it broadens the mind. **20–21** Perhaps you need to abandon something which is of little or no further use – holding on to it may not work out well. **KEY DATES: HIGHS 14–15** With positive things happening professionally, certain people may be glad to assist you. **LOWS 27–28** You might run out of energy all too suddenly; don't try to be all things to all people and take care over which tasks you choose to take on.

MARCH: MAIN TRENDS: 6–7 Plough through problems in relationships – although they are tested, if they are strong they will weather the storm. **17–18** You could benefit from keeping a lower professional profile; you may feel isolated but this can be advantageous. **20–21** A change for the better may come from getting to grips with certain facts and figures in the workplace, even if they seem overwhelming at first. **KEY DATES: HIGHS 13–14** A developing project may be ready to bear fruit in your life. **LOWS 26–28** Significant information may fail to turn up as expected; be wary of being led up the garden path.

APRIL: MAIN TRENDS: 1–2 Planets favouring intimate, affectionate relationships mean that you should now get the best from your love life. **20–21** If you need to make a good impression on someone, be sure to arrange an encounter during this influential period. **26–27** Concentrate your energies on the home – this may be a fairly nostalgic period when the past assumes enormous importance. **KEY DATES: HIGHS 9–11** If you are brave enough to be bold you may reap unexpected rewards. **LOWS 23–24** This influence tests your capacity to cope and you should soon realise what you can handle and what you can't.

MAY: MAIN TRENDS: 13–15 A challenging phase in your personal life looks likely – prioritise and eschew other ideas to keep things streamlined. **22–23** A great time to meet interesting, dynamic people. Your personal magnetism attracts you to others and likewise them to you. **24–25** Trends favour time spend outdoors – you may well find the weird and wonderful on your travels and the more you expand the better. **KEY DATES: HIGHS 7–8** A small, calculated risk may prove lucrative. You enjoy physical strength now, too. **LOWS 20–21** If you experience a personal let down take care not to overreact to the disappointment.

JUNE: MAIN TRENDS: 13–14 Matters at work proceed smoothly, but much now depends on the friendly assistance you can enlist. **21–22** Trends indicate that you will be rather disorganised now, and finding tasks overwhelming. Focus on the important issues and leave the rest for later. **29–30** Family concerns may assume top priority, as you are likely to want to stay at home and focus on your nearest and dearest. **KEY DATES: HIGHS 3–4; 30** With self determination there is nothing you cannot achieve – Lady Luck may lend a hand, too. **LOWS 16–17** Prepare to assert some self-discipline in order to clear up some unfinished business.

JULY: MAIN TRENDS: 3–4 Certain practical elements of daily life may break down and the need for renewal or repair may be evident. Patience is called for! **10–11** Trends now make you strong and capable, and your ability to attract the good things of life will not go unnoticed. **22–23** While it's good to get things done by being sure-footed and single-minded, you should also avoid any impulsive or rash decisions. **KEY DATES: HIGHS 1–2; 27–29** Make the most of new challenges and forge new beginnings if the opportunity arises. **LOWS 14–15** As the planetary forces around you slow down, go with the flow and take things gently also.

AUGUST: MAIN TRENDS: 6–7 This should be a rewarding time for partnerships, even if you find yourself playing the go-between or negotiator. **13–14** There is scope for progress as the wheels turn faster at work and you, in turn, enjoy high energy levels which enables you to keep up the pace. **22–23** Show off a little and use your powers of persuasion to get the most from life. Take care not to put anyone off, though! **KEY DATES: HIGHS 24–25** This trend may kick-start an important initiative as your positive efforts reach a climax. **LOWS 10–11** Watch out for some booby traps on the road to progress – they could undo what you have achieved thus far.

SEPTEMBER: MAIN TRENDS: 5–6 An excellent opportunity to seek co-operation with others. Now is the time to join forces with others and work as a team. **9–10** Another great time for surrounding yourself with friends. If you're looking for a little romance today you may well find it! **23–24** Passionate in your search for the truth, don't be afraid to get straight to the point. Clear out any deadwood, too. **KEY DATES: HIGHS 21–22** A time for thinking big and to initiate important projects of any kind. **LOWS 7–8** Your ability to take the initiative now seems to be undermined. Instead of worrying about this, relax and lie low for a while.

OCTOBER: MAIN TRENDS: 10–11 A reassuring time when it comes to domestic matters; you may find the outside world has little to offer and prefer hearth and home. **23–24** You should now have a clearer idea of which way the wind is blowing when it comes to important objectives, but defer decisions for the time being. **29–30** A change for the better may come from a social development. You thrive in situations where you can exchange personal ideas with new acquaintances. **KEY DATES: HIGHS 17–19** Make an early start and you should complete things quickly. **LOWS 4–5; 31** You may feel a little overtaxed, if not exhausted, so get some rest.

NOVEMBER: MAIN TRENDS: 11–12 Consolidate recent advances or successes you've made. Financial developments may lead to some significant new gains. **16–17** You may be ready for a change of scenery and to expand your horizons; make the most of this mood and seek out variety just for its own sake. **22–23** You seem to be at the focal point of social activity and can get along with everyone famously – some may want to be in your good books! **KEY DATES: HIGHS 14–15** Professional issues ought to go well and you may find someone in a position of authority an enormous help. **LOWS 1; 27–28** You may not see good results as quickly as you'd like, but don't try to hurry things along. Accept that this is a time to rest and recharge your batteries.

DECEMBER: MAIN TRENDS: 2–3 With strong creative abilities you can accomplish a great deal in your career that would otherwise have been difficult. **14–15** A favourable time for conversations and daily comings and goings when innovative, interesting and inventive ideas may strike you. **21–22** New opportunities may seem to be a tall order but you must decide whether the risk is worth the changes they can bring. **KEY DATES: HIGHS 11–13** The best time to make fresh starts and take a little chance as long as you have thought it through. **LOWS 25–26** Christmas offers the perfect opportunity to enjoy some self-indulgence!

PISCES BORN PEOPLE
Birthdays: 20 February to 20 March inclusive
Planets: Jupiter, Neptune. Birthstone: Bloodstone. Lucky day: Thursday

Keynote for the Year: *Take any opportunity for long-distance travel and to generally widen your horizons this year. This is how you make your world bigger and better!*

JANUARY: MAIN TRENDS: 11–12 This trend empowers you with a little more zest than usual and gives you the opportunity to make progress on a pet project. **18–19** A peak in material and financial matters helps you get the best out of situations at work. Also a day for treating yourself to a little of what you fancy! **22–23** If you need to make a judgement call keep an open mind and look closely at all the details involved. A hectic time at work also looks likely. **KEY DATES: HIGHS 20–21** Trends give you a boost and help your plans to turn out just as expected. **LOWS 5–7** Prepare for some personal disappointments that are no one's fault.

FEBRUARY: MAIN TRENDS: 10–11 This influence may help you develop new and exciting ideas – and provide the means to put them into practice. **14–15** Pleasurable influences over your domestic life now make this a wonderful day to relax quietly at home or perhaps to re-live the past. **20–21** Day-to-day life keeps you on the go but beware of trying to expand a project beyond its reasonable limits. **KEY DATES: HIGHS 16–18** A period when you should be full of optimism and high spirits – justifiably so! **LOWS 2–3** Try to keep a calm sense of perspective if sensitive and personal matters test your circumstances and sense of purpose.

MARCH: MAIN TRENDS: 6–7 Use your winning ways and the strength of your personal popularity to put your creative ideas to practical use today. **18–19** Emotionally deep relationships come into focus now, and a heart-to-heart could help you put certain matters into context. **20–21** Domestic life is now positively highlighted – seek out old friends and acquaintances to re-live old memories. **KEY DATES: HIGHS 15–17** Your confidence grows as planetary forces help you to get what you want. **LOWS 1–2; 29–30** An emotionally challenging time when setbacks may occur – put key issues on the back burner and relax.

APRIL: MAIN TRENDS: 1–2 Make an early start on tasks that need your attention and don't be afraid to implement changes if they are needed. **20–21** Try not to jump to conclusions before you have all the salient facts, especially with colleagues. **24–25** Rid yourself of things in your life that have outlived their usefulness, but don't turn away from anything that may just need repair. **KEY DATES: HIGHS 12–13** Your competitive instincts are enhanced and this is the perfect time to devote to money-making or even creative disciplines. **LOWS 25–26** During this planetary lull don't try to go too far, too fast.

MAY: MAIN TRENDS: 13–15 An appropriate time for finding solutions to problems, especially in a financial or work matter. **19–20** You see clearly towards the important goals ahead of you and have what it takes to push through your ambitions. **21–22** Don't expect to get all your own way with your partner – major compromises may be necessary to preserve the status quo. **KEY DATES: HIGHS 9–11** With energy to spare you should get a lot done as the impulse for progress is very powerful. **LOWS 22–23** Delays of various kinds are to be expected now and could test your patience; stay calm and ride out the trend.

JUNE: MAIN TRENDS: 13–14 You may get the chance to improve your popularity rating as trends make you attractive to others and in the mood to socialise. **21–22** Perhaps you are putting over your points of view rather forcefully. Beware the tendency to speak first and ask questions later. **29–30** A good time to work with others towards a common goal. Friends are generally co-operative and you operate best in a partnership. **KEY DATES: HIGHS 5–7** Lady Luck lends you a helping hand with the choices you make! **LOWS 18–20** Prepare to feel lacking in energy and make this a quiet period if you can.

JULY: MAIN TRENDS: 1–2 You may have to deal with potentially deceptive people and confusion may consequently reign. Keep your wits sharp to avoid this situation. **10–11** The planets may lead situations to conspire against you so don't expect any fantastic progress at work or at home just for now. **22–23** The way ahead becomes clearer as you tidy up outstanding minor tasks with speed and efficiency. **KEY DATES: HIGHS 3–4** There should be very little to stand in your way, and keeping up a high profile may have untold benefits. **LOWS 16–17** Let go of whatever isn't working and start again but not, perhaps, until this low patch is over.

AUGUST: MAIN TRENDS: 6–7 You may make a decisive breakthrough in something you've been recently struggling with. Put your best foot forward. **10–11** Trends bring a financial boost under which there are gains to be made, or maybe even unexpected money at your disposal. **23–24** Don't downgrade yourself or allow others to impose upon you. You will do best to retreat from the world for a little while. **KEY DATES: HIGHS 26–28** The planets should throw some useful assistance with major plans and projects your way. **LOWS 12–13** At your most sluggish time of the month the best idea is to get a couple of early nights.

SEPTEMBER: MAIN TRENDS: 6–7 Stay on the move – you spread good vibes and people you meet feel energised by contact with you. **11–12** A nice time for all domestic activities and loved ones seem to have your best interests at heart. Why not enjoy entertaining at home? **25–26** An in-depth talk with a colleague might be just what the doctor ordered; stay in touch with what's going on in the world to avoid missing something vital. **KEY DATES: HIGHS 23–24** Current planetary influences bring quite a lot of luck to your daily life. Make the most of it! **LOWS 9–10** Now is the time to take care of routine tasks and not for far-reaching schemes.

OCTOBER: MAIN TRENDS: 10–11 Your strength lies in your ability to get what you want during this lucrative period when your energy seems indefatigable. **23–24** Work trends are steady – and you don't mind being in a demanding role if it means earning extra money. **30–31** A time to encounter the weird and wonderful, so long as you get out and about in wide open spaces. **KEY DATES: HIGHS 20–21** You can expect your plans for expansion to take off – why not be the eternal optimist? **LOWS 6–7** Try to have faith in life even if things don't go your way.

NOVEMBER: MAIN TRENDS: 11–12 Places of entertainment and leisure hold much in store for you as it's time to get your social and romantic life organised! **14–15** Old friends may give you cause to consider their real value to you now – is it the right time to say goodbye? **22–23** Discuss your career plans with others even if they won't agree with everything you propose. A leading role elsewhere may be in the offing. **KEY DATES: HIGHS 16–18** Thinking big pays off at this time which is likely to be a very 'go ahead' period for your personal plans, dreams and schemes. **LOWS 2–3; 29–30** Don't squander any opportunity for success now – but do take things easy.

DECEMBER: MAIN TRENDS: 2–3 A very beneficial trend for all forms of physical activity. Financially you may reap some rewards, too. **12–13** Emotional issues arise and elements of your personal life become uncertain; talk things over with a loved one to help you keep things in perspective. **21–22** Family life now provides some of your most rewarding times – a good influence for entertaining at home or doing some DIY. **KEY DATES: HIGHS 14–15** A dynamic period when you can create excitement and attract some good will your way. **LOWS 1; 27–28** Keep a low profile, Pisces, finish off any outstanding jobs and you'll feel better about yourself.

200-year Perpetual Calendar

Do you know on which day of the week you or your friends were born? You may remember that World War II was declared on Sunday, 3 September 1939, but on which day did World War I start?

This calendar, created originally by C. E. Forsythe, allows you to find the weekday for any date from 1850 to 2050. You will find it useful and informative and very simple to use. Just follow the instructions to check birthdays, events and special occasions.

- Find the year in Table A.
- Follow across on the same line to Table B and select the number under the relevant month.
- Add this number to the date.
- Look up this number in Table C and follow across to the left to find the day of the week.

Table A / **Table B**

Year	Year	Year	Year	Year	Year	Year	Year	Jan	Feb	Mar	Apri	May	June	July	Aug	Sept	Oct	Nov	Dec
1850	1878		1918	1946	1974	2002	2030	2	5	5	1	3	6	1	4	0	2	5	0
1851	1879		1919	1947	1975	2003	2031	3	6	6	2	4	0	2	5	1	3	6	1
* 1852	1880		1920	1948	1976	2004	2032	4	0	1	4	6	2	4	0	3	5	1	3
1853	1881		1921	1949	1977	2005	2033	6	2	2	5	0	3	5	1	4	6	2	4
1854	1882		1922	1950	1978	2006	2034	0	3	3	6	1	4	6	2	5	0	3	5
1855	1883		1923	1951	1979	2007	2035	1	4	4	0	2	5	0	3	6	1	4	6
* 1856	1884		1924	1952	1980	2008	2036	2	5	6	2	4	0	2	5	1	3	6	1
1857	1885		1925	1953	1981	2009	2037	4	0	0	3	5	1	3	6	2	4	0	2
1858	1886		1926	1954	1982	2010	2038	5	1	1	4	6	2	4	0	3	5	1	3
1859	1887		1927	1955	1983	2011	2039	6	2	2	5	0	3	5	1	4	6	2	4
* 1860	1888		1928	1956	1984	2012	2040	0	3	4	0	2	5	0	3	6	1	4	6
1861	1889	1901	1929	1957	1985	2013	2041	2	5	5	1	3	6	1	4	0	2	5	0
1862	1890	1902	1930	1958	1986	2014	2042	3	6	6	2	4	0	2	5	1	3	6	1
1863	1891	1903	1931	1959	1987	2015	2043	4	0	0	3	5	1	3	6	2	4	0	2
* 1864	1892	1904	1932	1960	1988	2016	2044	5	1	2	5	0	3	5	1	4	6	2	4
1865	1893	1905	1933	1961	1989	2017	2045	0	3	3	6	1	4	6	2	5	0	3	5
1866	1894	1906	1934	1962	1990	2018	2046	1	4	4	0	2	5	0	3	6	1	4	6
1867	1895	1907	1935	1963	1991	2019	2047	2	5	5	1	3	6	1	4	0	2	5	0
* 1868	1896	1908	1936	1964	1992	2020	2048	3	6	0	3	5	1	3	6	2	4	0	2
1869	1897	1909	1937	1965	1993	2021	2049	5	1	1	4	6	2	4	0	3	5	1	3
1870	1898	1910	1938	1966	1994	2022	2050	6	2	2	5	0	3	5	1	4	6	2	4
1871	1899	1911	1939	1967	1995	2023		0	3	3	6	1	4	6	2	5	0	3	5
* 1872		1912	1940	1968	1996	2024		1	4	5	1	3	6	1	4	0	2	5	0
1873		1913	1941	1969	1997	2025		3	6	6	2	4	0	2	5	1	3	6	1
1874		1914	1942	1970	1998	2026		4	0	0	3	5	1	3	6	2	4	0	2
1875		1915	1943	1971	1999	2027		5	1	1	4	6	2	4	0	3	5	1	3
* 1876		1916	1944	1972	2000	2028		6	2	3	6	1	4	6	2	5	0	3	5
1877	1900	1917	1945	1973	2001	2029		1	4	4	0	2	5	0	3	6	1	4	6

Table C

Sunday	1	8	15	22	29	36
Monday	2	9	16	23	30	37
Tuesday	3	10	17	24	31	
Wednesday	4	11	18	25	32	
Thursday	5	12	19	26	33	
Friday	6	13	20	27	34	
Saturday	7	14	21	28	35	

* Years on the lines to the right of the asterisks are leap years.

> **Example: 3 March 1896**
> March 1896 = 0
> Date = 3
> 0 + 3 = 3 so it fell on a Tuesday
>
> **Example: 27 July 2005**
> July 2005 = 5
> Date = 27
> 5 + 27 = 32 so it will fall on a Wednesday

Best Sowing and Planting Times for the Garden in 2018

WHEN TO PLANT OR SOW BY THE MOON TO GET THE BEST RESULTS

Peas, beans, flowering vegetables and plants which produce fruit above the ground should always be sown under a waxing Moon (the period from New Moon to Full). Potatoes and root crops should always be sown when the Moon is low and below the Earth. If you sow, plant or re-pot at the times set out below, it is reasonably certain you will have really fine results. The times are Greenwich Mean Time. Allowances must be made for British Summer Time.

Month	Day	Planting Times		
JANUARY	1, 2, 3	8.30 to 11.05 am	2.20 to 3.15 pm	
	16, 17, 18	8.20 to 11.45 am	1.15 to 2.30 pm	
FEBRUARY	1, 2, 3	8.40 to 11.05 am	1.00 to 3.05 pm	
	14, 15, 16	8.05 to 10.20 am	1.05 to 3.00 pm	
		Begin sowing legumes, leaf vegetables and root vegetables. Delay beetroot until the weather is mild. Cut early kidney potatoes for seed and use a heater or heat mats to get them started.		
MARCH	1, 2, 3	8.05 to 11.50 am	1.15 to 2.20 pm	3.15 to 4.05 pm
	16, 17, 18	8.05 to 11.50 am	1.15 to 2.20 pm	3.15 to 4.05 pm
		Planting and sowing into the ground can begin this month. Sow asparagus, celery, brassicas, and continue with root vegetables and legumes. Cabbages, onion sets and sea-kale may be planted out.		
APRIL	15, 16, 17	7.15 to 11.30 am	1.15 to 2.30 pm	4.15 to 5.05 pm
	28, 29, 30	7.30 to 11.15 am	12.20 to 2.25 pm	3.55 to 5.30 pm
		Sowing of tomatoes and peppers can begin indoors. Continue sowing legumes, brassicas and leaf vegetables for the main summer crop. Plant out rhubarb, artichokes, asparagus and small salad vegetables. Tie up lettuce and in dry weather water seed in beds.		
MAY	14, 15, 16	7.10 to 11.00 am	12.40 to 2.50 pm	4.15 to 5.55 pm
	27, 28, 29	7.30 to 11.05 am	12.20 to 2.55 pm	4.05 to 5.40 pm
		Sow cucumber, dwarf bean, runner beans and courgettes and a full crop of kidney beans. Transplant cabbage, winter greens, cauliflower and celery seedlines. Hoe and stake peas, water newly planted crops.		
JUNE	12, 13, 14	7.05 to 11.00 am	12.30 to 3.20 pm	4.15 to 5.50 pm
	27, 28, 29	7.15 to 11.05 am	12.40 to 2.20 pm	4.20 to 5.30 pm
		Top beans and peas to assist the filling of the pods. Set kidney beans. Thin out onions, leeks, parsnips and early turnips. Plant tomatoes and peppers outdoors. Water all crops well during dry spells.		
JULY	12, 13, 14	7.15 to 11.15 am	12.30 to 3.50 pm	4.20 to 6.15 pm
	26, 27, 28	7.55 to 10.55 am	12.30 to 3.20 pm	4.30 to 7.05 pm
		Plant out the last of the brassicas and cabbages and earth up celery. Lift full-grown winter onions and new potatoes. Pick vine crops as they ripen to encourage new fruit.		
AUGUST	10, 11, 12	7.15 to 11.05 am	12.30 to 3.05 pm	5.55 to 7.55 pm
	25, 26, 27	7.15 to 11.00 am	12.30 to 2.50 pm	6.05 to 8.05 pm
		Sow early cabbages and parsley for the succeeding year, also spinach, broccoli and cauliflower to stand the winter and transplant seedlings. Continue to pick legumes and vine crops as they ripen.		
SEPTEMBER	8, 9, 15	6.40 to 11.30 am	1.00 to 4.30 pm	6.05 to 7.45 pm
	24, 25, 26	7.15 to 11.30 am	1.15 to 4.05 pm	5.40 to 7.00 pm
		Plant cabbages, broccoli, cauliflowers, leeks, celery. Pull onions if tips appear to be drying. Sow winter lettuce. Store potatoes and apples properly for winter.		
OCTOBER	8, 9, 15	7.40 am to 12.00 pm	1.05 to 3.30 pm	4.55 to 6.30 pm
	23, 24, 25	7.55 to 11.15 am	1.05 to 3.45 pm	4.25 to 5.30 pm
		Plant some radishes, early cabbages, cauliflower, and some herbs like mint, thyme and tarragon in frames for winter use. Sow the last winter lettuce. Harvest crops before any risk of frost.		
NOVEMBER	6, 7, 8	7.50 am to 12.15 pm	2.20 to 4.30 pm	
	22, 23, 24	8.45 to 11.50 am	2.15 to 3.55 pm	
		Dig ground once crops are carried off and there is no intention to plant again until spring. Shallots are readily propagated by offcuts. Clear fallen leaves quickly and dispose of diseased plants.		
DECEMBER	6, 7, 8	9.15 am to 1.05 pm	2.20 to 3.10 pm	
	21, 22, 23	9.10 am to 12.50 pm	1.55 to 3.00 pm	
		Earth up celery. Sow small salad vegetables in warm borders covered with mats.		

Racing with the Jockeys in 2018

ASTROLOGICAL POINTERS TO POSSIBLE WINNING PERIODS

The astrologically compiled dates below are presented to race-goers in the hope that they will point the way to some successful winning periods during the 2018 racing season. Specially recommended = sr.

FAVOURABLE PERIODS FOR FLAT-RACE JOCKEYS

A. KIRBY: Born 22 August 1988. Likely to do best on 3-year-olds in the mid part of the season. His favourable periods are: 16, 18, 25 March; 15–20, 27–30 April (27 sr); 2–5, 15–17, 24 May (15, 17, sr); 4, 12–19, 22–25 June; 1, 7, 17, 22–28 July (7, 22 sr); 1–3, 5–9, 19–25, 27, 31 August (19, 22 sr); 2, 11, 15–17, 25 September (25 sr); 13, 19, 21–26, 29, 31 October (19 sr); 1–2, 14–17, 28–30 November.

L. MORRIS: Born 20 October 1988. Left-hand courses in the north may bring his best victories this season. His favourable periods are: 2, 15, 20, 24–25 March; 1, 8–10, 18–22, 25 April (18, 25 sr); 1–2, 7–10, 18–24 May; 6, 12–13, 22–25 June; 2–5, 14–20, 25–27 July; 1–8, 14–15, 25–26 August; 1–2, 7–8, 16–18, 22–24 October; 2–7, 11, 15–17, 22–24 November (22–24 sr).

S. DE SOUSA: Born 31 December 1980. Ought to be noted this season in the south, in particular on the longer tracks. His favourable periods are: 6–8, 13–14, 19–21, 25–27 March; 16–18, 24–30 April; 3–5, 8, 17–21, 30 May (3–5 sr); 7–11, 18, 21–25 June; 1, 5, 12–14, 22–29 July (12, 29 sr); 1–2, 18, 20–24 August; 2–7, 16–17, 19–20, 28 September (19, 28 sr); 6–8, 12–14, 17, 23–31 October (12–14 sr); 3–4, 7–10, 14, 23–26, 30 November (14 sr).

J. FANNING: Born 24 September 1970. When it comes to sprinters this season, the Irish jockey is likely to do particularly well late in the year. His favourable periods are: 1, 3–4, 16–18, 20–22 March (18 sr); 1, 4–6, 12, 28–29 April; 5, 11–13, 24–28 May (11–13 sr); 2–3, 14–15, 22–23, 28–30 June; 4–7, 18, 20–25, 28–29 July (20–25 sr); 1, 4–6, 15–18, 19–21, 24, 31 August (19–21 sr); 5–9, 13, 19, 21–22, 28–30 September; 3, 9, 13–14, 24 October; 6–7, 16, 28–30 November.

FAVOURABLE PERIODS FOR NATIONAL HUNT JOCKEYS

T. SCUDAMORE: Born 22 May 1982. He could do particularly well with 3-year-old hurdlers in the Midlands this year. His favourable periods are: 14–15, 19, 21–24, 31 January; 1, 6–11, 21–26 February; 1–5, 12–18, 25 March (25 sr); 9–12, 17, 22–23 April (22 sr); 1–5, 16, 25–26 May (5, 26 sr); 8, 17, 20, 24–29 June; 1–8, 15–21, 30–31 July; 11–12, 24–28 August (24–28 sr); 3–4, 9–11, 28–30 September (3–4 sr); 5–12, 18, 25–26 October (18 sr); 1–3, 21, 26–28 November (26–28 sr); 5–8, 10, 22 December.

R. JOHNSON: Born 27 July 1977. May do very well on weight-for-age races this year whatever the venue. His favourable periods are: 4, 17–20, 26 January; 3, 16–17, 21–22 February; 12, 20, 23–26 March; 1–7, 20, 22–23 April (22–23 sr); 3–10, 16–17, 28 May (3–10 sr); 2–5, 9–14, 24, 30 June (24 sr); 10–11, 15–17, 23–27 July (15–17 sr); 2–4, 7–10, 23–25 August; 2–3, 13–15, 30 September; 1–2, 14–17, 31 October; 2–3, 8–10, 21, 25–29 November (8–10 sr); 2, 5–7, 13 December.

S. TWISTON DAVIES: Born 15 October 1992. Likely to have quite a good season on mares, especially at northern race tracks. His favourable periods are: 4–7, 20, 28 January; 1–2, 16–18, 22–24 February; 4, 8–9, 27–30 March; 5, 9–10, 19–24, 30 April; 8, 14–15, 23–24, 31 May; 1, 12, 21–24 June; 6–8, 11–14, 22 July (11–14, 22 sr); 3–6, 17–18, 29–31 August; 2, 5–10, 24 September; 11, 26–28, 31 October; 3–4, 14–15, 28–29 November (28–29 sr); 6–10, 13–22, 28–31 December.

Racing with the Trainers in 2018

ASTROLOGICAL POINTERS TO POSSIBLE WINNING PERIODS

The astrologically compiled dates below are presented to race-goers in the hope that they will point the way to some successful winning periods during the 2018 racing season. Specially recommended = sr.

FAVOURABLE PERIODS FOR FLAT-RACE TRAINERS

J. GOSDEN: Born 30 March 1951. Likely to do best with mares and should be noted at northern venues with 2-year-old horses. His favourable periods are: 14–16, 20–22, 29 March (14–16 sr); 6–9, 11–12, 22, 24, 27–30 April (27–30 sr); 2–5, 13–14, 23, 29 May (13–14 sr); 1, 10–12, 15–18 June; 1–2, 6, 11–12, 14–16, 29–31 July (14–16 sr); 1–3, 8–10, 13–16, 24 August (13–16 sr); 7–8, 12–15, 24, 29 September (7–8, 29 sr); 4, 6, 11, 21–22, 27 October (6, 27 sr); 1, 9–10 November.

R. HANNON Jnr: Born 21 November 1975. To be followed this season with his 2- and 4-year-olds, in races at southern courses. His favourable periods are: 1–2, 11–12, 24–29 March (24 sr); 1, 13–17, 22, 24 April (22 sr); 1–3, 6, 21, 27 May (1–3 sr); 1, 7–10, 15, 20, 25 June; 6–9, 18, 23–31 July; 3, 11–17, 23–27 August (23–27 sr); 1, 4–8, 12–13, 24–27 September; 4–11, 17, 22, 27 October; 2, 4–7, 15, 24–26 November (24–26 sr).

C. APPLEBY: Born 5 July 1975. Could easily succeed best in northern handicaps this year on 4-year-olds. His favourable periods are: 5, 7, 24–28 March (5, 24 sr); 4–8, 14–17, 21–24, 30 April; 2–6, 8–10, 27–28 May (28 sr); 4–5, 17–18, 22–25 June; 1–2, 9, 15, 28–31 July; 2–5, 12–16, 20, 28 August (20, 28 sr); 1–3, 8–12, 15–17, 29–30 September (15–17 sr); 2–4, 16–17, 24–29 October (16 sr); 3–11, 20–25 November.

FAVOURABLE PERIODS FOR NATIONAL HUNT TRAINERS

P. NICHOLLS: Born 17 April 1962. Could succeed much better with colts, especially in any handicapped races this year. His favourable periods are: 17–23, 31 January (23 sr); 8, 10, 12–15, 28 February (12, 28 sr); 15–16, 20–21, 28–29 March (28 sr); 2, 15–16, 21–25, 28–29 April (2 sr); 5, 19–23, 30 May (30 sr); 9–10, 17–26 June; 4–8, 11–13, 28–29 July; 1, 15–16, 31 August; 10–11, 20, 28–30 September; 9–11, 16, 22, 25, 30–31 October (16 sr); 1–2, 10–12, 15, 26 November (2, 26 sr); 9, 11, 15–18, 21 December (18 sr).

P. J. HOBBS: Born 26 July 1955. Should do well especially early in the season, perhaps with 2- or 3-year-olds. His favourable periods are: 5–6, 12, 25, 31 January; 15–19, 22–26 February; 1–9, 18–19, 28–31 March; 2–4, 18, 28–30 April (28–30 sr); 1–3, 8–9, 13–19, 28–31 May; 1–5, 11–15, 23–30 June; 1, 8–10, 22–25, 30–31 July; 3, 6, 15–18, 29–30 August; 1–4, 15–19, 22–23 September; 2, 12, 15, 29 October (2, 12 sr); 3–5, 18–22, 27–30 November; 10–13, 14–19, 28 December.

JONJO O'NEILL: Born 13 April 1952. Should do particularly well on the longer courses down south this year. His favourable periods are: 2, 14–15, 19–20, 26–30 January; 7–8, 15–22, 27 February; 9, 12–13, 25 March; 12, 18–20, 29–30 April; 8, 20–23, 28 May (20 sr); 6–7, 14–17, 22–26, 30 June; 3–5, 9–13, 27–31 July; 2, 15–16, 25, 27 August; 1–4, 16–19, 22, 28 September (1–4 sr); 4–5, 15–16, 28–31 October; 2–4, 10, 17, 28–30 November; 2–5, 9–11, 27–29 December (2–5 sr).

Football Pools Forecast for 2018

This forecast, based on a combination of planetary indications and team colours, lists the teams likely to draw on the dates given, or within two days either side. No claims to infallibility are made and readers should use their own judgement, but forecasts may help them in the final selection.

6 January
Everton, Chelsea, Mansfield, Rotherham, Manchester Utd

13 January
Ipswich, Blackpool, Motherwell, Leicester City

20 January
Aston Villa, Birmingham, Bristol City, Chelsea

27 January
Reading, Nottingham Forest, Bolton, Liverpool, Swindon

3 February
Liverpool, Chelsea, Crystal Palace, Watford

10 February
Tottenham Hotspur, Hull City, Hearts, Leeds, Sunderland

17 February
West Bromwich Albion, Shrewsbury Town, Celtic, Charlton Athletic

24 February
Newcastle Utd, Coventry City, Sheffield Wednesday, Kilmarnock

3 March
Peterborough, Colchester, Wolves, Blackburn, Burnley

10 March
Motherwell, Sunderland, Bury, Watford, Fulham

17 March
Charlton Athletic, Tottenham Hotspur, Hamilton, Southampton

24 March
Leicester City, West Ham, Carlisle, Bury, Preston

31 March
Sunderland, Bury, Derby County, MK Dons

7 April
Bolton, Peterborough, Wolves, Bradford, Blackpool

14 April
Middlesbrough, Scunthorpe,

Sheffield Wednesday, West Bromwich Albion

21 April
Exeter, Crystal Palace, Manchester City, Bournemouth

28 April
Dundee, Middlesbrough, Bolton, Fulham

5 May
Yeovil Town, Stoke, Birmingham, MK Dons

6 May
Hearts, Doncaster, Stoke, Southampton, Manchester Utd

12 May
Plymouth, West Ham, Chelsea, Oxford United

19 May
Oldham Athletic, Doncaster, Leicester City, Fleetwood

11 August
Ipswich Town, Preston, Blackburn, Blackpool

18 August
Hull City, Aston Villa, West Bromwich Albion, Wigan, Sunderland

25 August
Liverpool, Watford, Ipswich Town, Everton

1 September
Bristol Rovers, Newcastle Utd, Yeovil Town, Colchester

8 September
Fleetwood, Bolton, Crystal Palace, Manchester Utd, Hull City

15 September
Celtic, Arsenal, Birmingham, Burnley, Fulham

22 September
Kilmarnock, Celtic, QPR, Swansea City, Blackburn

29 September
Leeds, St Mirren, Inverness,

Manchester City, Blackpool

6 October
Tranmere Rovers, Falkirk, Grimsby, Birmingham, Carlisle

13 October
Hull City, St Johnstone, Swansea City, Blackpool

20 October
Newcastle Utd, Stoke City, Manchester Utd, Bolton, Celtic

27 October
Coventry City, Derby County, Birmingham, Aston Villa

3 November
Scunthorpe, Arsenal, Port Vale, Liverpool, Rochdale

10 November
Norwich City, Crystal Palace, Scunthorpe, Preston

17 November
Watford, Nottingham Forest, Dunfermline, Southampton

24 November
Millwall, Peterborough, Manchester City, West Ham

1 December
Middlesbrough, Rangers, Sheffield, Swansea City, West Bromwich Albion

8 December
Wrexham, Dundee, Manchester Utd, Nottingham Forest, Burnley

15 December
Stoke City, Hamilton, Fulham, Cardiff City, Blackburn

22 December
Bristol Rovers, Newcastle Utd, Burnley, Brighton, Sheffield United

29 December
Crystal Palace, Hartlepool, Blackburn, Hull City, Leicester

Who was Old Moore?

Francis Moore, a Shropshire lad, was born in 1657. Despite his humble beginnings he taught himself to read and write and developed an interest in medicine, which at the time was heavily dependent on astrology. Like Dick Whittington, he eventually made his way to London to make his fortune. He worked with the eminent astrologer John Partridge, and having added medical astrology to his skills, Dr Moore set up his own business in Southwark. Good at his profession, he was privileged to attain the status of Physician to the Court of King Charles II.

Moore launched his first black and white broadsheet in 1697. By 1700, with his Court connections, he had compiled the first of his famous *Vox Stellarum* series – *The Voice of the Stars*. The predictions were probably a spin off from his astrological calculations and were included to increase the Almanack sales to the wider public. For those unable to read, special symbols were printed alongside certain days to indicate the importance of the event. When he died in 1715 Moore's Almanack was taken over by the Worshipful Company of Liveried Stationers who continued to publish it until 1911 when the House of Foulsham bought the copyright. It has been published every year since 1697, earning it a place in the *Guinness Book of Records*.

Today, a team of astrologers represent Old Moore working 18 months ahead of actual events. Year after year, they describe the direction that the UK and the world will take focusing on the key players and issues. There isn't another seer in the world who can claim the duration of accuracy that is published under the by-line Dr Francis Moore.

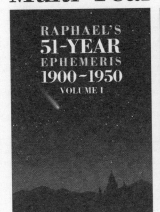

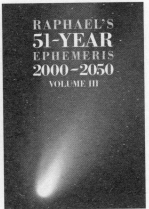

Angler's Guide for 2018

THE BEST DATES AND TECHNIQUES FOR SUCCESSFUL FISHING

JANUARY: Sport can be hard due to low temperatures, so stick to deeper water on rivers and lakes. Backwaters are a good bet when main rivers are flooded: try float or leger tactics in slack water swims. Shoaling cod may be caught from the beaches, especially in Scotland, on casting gear but they will soon thin out as temperatures rise. **Best days:** 1 (pm), 6 (pm), 9, 11 (am), 18 (pm), 23, 24, 26 (am), 30, 31 (pm).

FEBRUARY: Predator fishing offers the best action with pike, perch and zander all possible on fish baits, but scale down your tackle if the temperature plummets. Big chub can also be had on leger tactics. Spring salmon on the cards for some anglers, but beach rods will have to work harder for their catches. Flatties will still feature, although bigger fish can be had when afloat. **Best days:** 3 (am), 5, 13 (pm), 15 (am), 19, 20 (pm), 21, 27 (am).

MARCH: The freshwater river season closes this month, but almost all commercial still waters will stay open. If mild weather comes early, head for sheltered lakes which can produce superb mixed catches of roach, bream, carp and even tench. Trout anglers head for deep, still waters from the 15th. **Best days:** 2, 4 (pm), 8, 9 (am), 15, 19 (am), 21, 22, 25 (am).

APRIL: Beach anglers can enjoy the spring run of codling, while those fishing wrecks can expect bumper hauls of pollack, ling and occasional big cod on artificial baits. Ray fishing good, especially in the Solent. Most flies will take trout on still waters but a more careful approach is needed in rivers. **Best days:** 1, 4 (am), 9, 12 (am), 18 (pm), 19, 20 (am), 24, 27 (pm).

MAY: Crab baits worthy for early school bass, flounder and eel, while ragworm and lugworm will take their fair share of plaice in harbours and estuaries. Still-water trout should respond to warmer weather and can be taken on floating lines. Carp will be the bulk of catches for commercial still-water anglers. **Best days:** 2, 3, 5 (am), 11, 13 (pm), 17, 18 (pm), 24, 26 (am).

JUNE: The Glorious 16th will enable specimen tench, carp and bream to be targeted with big baits on both float and leger tackle. Rivers with more pace should provide excellent catches of roach and chub. Beach anglers will find bass more widespread, while their boat counterparts can expect mackerel – the perfect bait for shark and tope – which will start to show off many southern and Welsh ports. **Best days:** 1, 5, 6 (pm), 20, 21, 22 (am), 25, 26, 30 (pm).

JULY: Top sport on rivers and lakes with virtually all species responsive, mostly to particle baits such as corn, hemp and tares. Try swims with plenty of flow as fish, particularly barbel and bream, will be hungry for oxygen-rich water during hot weather. Evening sessions ideal for fly anglers pursuing trout. Shy mullet may be tempted during quiet days around harbours, and bass will be bigger. **Best days:** 11, 12 (pm), 15, 19 (am), 20, 21, 26, 30, 31 (pm).

AUGUST: Low oxygen levels suggest fishing either very early morning or evening periods. Sea anglers afloat can look forward to a multitude of species including bream, bass, pollack, conger and gurnard. Fresh fish baits and crab will outscore all others. **Best days:** 1, 3, 4 (pm), 10, 15, 16 (am), 23, 25, 26, 27 (am).

SEPTEMBER: Fish will have had time to feed well and big specimens can be expected. Barbel, roach, bream, tench and chub will all be at their optimum weight. Trout anglers may struggle to locate decent fish, although beach and boat rods will be hunting big bass with sand eel baits, crab or lures. **Best days:** 1, 2, 7 (pm), 12, 14 (am), 20 (pm), 28, 29, 30 (am).

OCTOBER: Cooler temperatures may mean slow sport on lakes, but rivers will be at their peak for roach, chub and dace on caster or maggot. Float tactics are good but don't discount leger or feeder gear. Beach anglers expect the first of the winter codling, where lugworm and squid will be top baits. Extra water may prompt decent catches of salmon for game anglers. **Best days:** 9, 10 (pm), 15, 16 (pm), 22, 25 (pm), 28, 29 (am).

NOVEMBER: With shorter days, codling will come closer inshore, especially at deeper venues such as steep beaches, harbour walls and piers. Bad weather may mean slower sport for coarse anglers, who need to scale down hooks and baits. Predator hunters can expect big pike on baits rather than lures. **Best days:** 5, 10, 11, 16 (am), 18, 19, 22 (am).

DECEMBER: A roving approach is best during colder weather. Try different swims on backwaters, where roach will take bread flake, and chub can be had on cheese paste, bread, worms and cockles. Pin baits hard to the bottom or let them roll in the flow. After a storm is ideal for targeting codling on beaches, when they attack food stirred up by rough weather. Try night sessions for greater success. **Best days:** 7, 8 (am), 12, 18, 19 (am), 20, 22 (pm), 30 (am).

Greyhound Racing Numbers for 2018

TRAP-NUMBER FORECASTS FOR POTENTIAL SUCCESS

Each area of the UK has a ruling planetary number and each month of 2018 has a prominent fortunate planetary number. This forecast is based on a combination of those numbers to provide a list of the most propitious dates for betting and the trap numbers most likely to be successful.

The table gives the main areas of the UK and under each monthly heading, the first column shows the best dates for betting, and the second, shaded column gives the trap numbers for the winner and the second dog.

Whilst making no claim to infallibility, this forecast should offer those who enjoy an occasional jaunt to greyhound race meetings a way of aligning their activities with the best planetary influences and potentially increasing their success rate.

MEETING	JAN		FEB		MAR		APRIL		MAY		JUNE		JULY		AUG		SEPT		OCT		NOV		DEC	
London	6–8	1 4	4–15	1 2	2–10	2 4	4–9	1 6	2–10	2 4	3–8	1 6	6–12	1 3	1–7	3 5	2–10	3 5	6–10	1 3	3–7	3 5	8–14	1 6
	18–25	1 6	20–25	1 3	22–28	5 6	19–25	3 4	24–30	3 5	22–29	5 6	17–24	5 6	24–30	1 5	24–30	1 5	20–25	4 5	19–28	2 4	16–22	1 4
Birmingham	4–12	1 6	3–13	4 6	3–9	3 4	8–12	3 5	4–16	3 6	1–9	2 4	2–12	1 4	3–12	2 5	4–9	1 3	3–10	3 6	8–14	2 6	7–13	4 5
	22–26	2 4	22–29	1 4	19–28	2 6	20–27	1 2	16–26	4 5	15–23	3 4	19–24	1 6	24–31	2 4	22–30	1 4	24–28	1 6	16–22	3 5	22–25	2 3
Manchester	2–4	1 2	3–14	2 3	8–12	3 4	5–9	3 5	3–8	2 4	8–10	4 6	3–6	1 6	9–14	2 6	7–14	1 4	3–11	2 6	8–14	3 6	4–9	2 4
	16–26	3 4	19–26	1 4	26–30	3 5	19–26	1 2	22–29	3 6	24–30	2 4	26–28	1 4	16–22	2 6	26–30	1 3	18–25	4 5	15–21	3 4	23–26	2 3
Newcastle	3–10	1 2	6–15	2 5	9–15	2 6	10–14	3 4	8–13	1 6	5–11	2 5	1–10	1 6	5–10	2 4	3–6	2 6	11–15	1 4	8–12	2 3	6–10	1 5
	18–26	5 6	22–26	1 5	26–31	3 4	24–30	2 5	19–22	3 6	22–28	4 5	22–26	2 6	24–29	2 4	17–25	1 3	22–27	3 5	24–31	1 4	21–26	2 3
Sheffield	5–9	3 4	4–12	3 4	2–8	2 4	2–4	3 6	3–8	4 5	7–12	1 6	2–8	1 3	7–12	2 3	2–10	1 5	4–7	1 6	10–14	1 3	4–10	2 3
	19–26	1 4	22–27	2 3	21–31	4 6	15–18	2 4	9–13	1 6	20–28	2 3	15–19	3 4	17–23	2 4	19–27	3 4	20–28	3 6	22–30	2 3	16–20	4 5
Wales	2–9	3 6	5–12	2 6	2–7	1 5	7–13	1 2	8–12	5 6	6–10	3 5	5–11	1 2	2–7	1 6	1–6	1 2	9–14	1 6	6–10	2 3	1–8	3 4
	21–30	1 4	20–23	1 2	17–24	3 4	19–27	2 6	22–28	1 5	16–20	4 6	16–23	2 6	18–23	4 5	20–27	2 5	24–31	3 4	17–22	2 6	19–24	3 5
South of England	3–8	2 4	6–12	1 3	7–12	2 5	12–15	1 2	3–9	3 5	1–8	2 3	2–8	3 4	6–12	2 6	8–13	3 5	3–9	1 6	4–10	2 3	7–11	1 5
	15–19	1 4	19–26	2 5	24–30	3 4	25–30	1 2	22–25	4 6	18–22	3 5	17–21	1 2	20–27	2 5	22–28	2 4	24–29	3 5	21–25	4 6	25–31	1 2

Lucky Dates to Play Bingo in 2018

CHECK YOUR ZODIAC SIGN FOR YOUR GOOD-LUCK TIMES

Aries (Birthdays 21 March to 20 April)
8 February to 2 April, 13 July to 24 August, 31 October to 28 November

❁

Taurus (Birthdays 21 April to 21 May)
18 February to 1 April, 20 July to 20 September, 14 November to 29 December

❁

Gemini (Birthdays 22 May to 21 June)
9 January to 1 March, 29 April to 2 July, 1 October to 4 December

❁

Cancer (Birthdays 22 June to 22 July)
22 March to 19 May, 2 July to 28 August, 19 November to 28 December

❁

Leo (Birthdays 23 July to 23 August)
4 February to 27 April, 20 June to 4 August, 23 October to 6 December

❁

Virgo (Birthdays 24 August to 23 September)
22 January to 7 March, 23 July to 4 September, 20 October to 31 December

❁

Libra (Birthdays 24 September to 23 October)
1 January to 1 March, 2 July to 1 September, 3 November to 21 December

❁

Scorpio (Birthdays 24 October to 22 November)
1 January to 4 March, 25 May to 31 July, 29 September to 25 November

❁

Sagittarius (Birthdays 23 November to 21 December)
13 February to 4 April, 13 June to 27 August, 2 October to 30 November

❁

Capricorn (Birthdays 22 December to 20 January)
1 February to 18 April, 28 June to 1 September, 15 November to 29 December

❁

Aquarius (Birthdays 21 January to 19 February)
2 January to 24 March, 28 May to 13 July, 30 September to 8 November

❁

Pisces (Birthdays 20 February to 20 March)
9 February to 8 April, 23 June to 2 August, 6 October to 17 December

Thunderball Astro-Guide for 2018

Thunderball forecasts are based on the power of the Sun and Jupiter in each zodiacal period. In a random draw there can be no guarantee, but these numbers may help to improve your chances. First, find your sun sign in the left-hand column. Then read across the first panel to select five numbers 1–39 for the main part of your entry. Then select one number from the second panel for the Thunderball.

Sign	Dates	Main numbers						Thunderball			
ARIES	21 MARCH TO 20 APRIL	2	8	19	34	35	38	1	5	9	13
TAURUS	21 APRIL TO 21 MAY	5	7	19	24	28	33	2	7	11	12
GEMINI	22 MAY TO 21 JUNE	10	11	23	26	29	34	3	6	8	10
CANCER	22 JUNE TO 22 JULY	3	5	17	18	29	39	7	8	12	13
LEO	23 JULY TO 23 AUGUST	2	8	13	20	22	32	2	5	6	11
VIRGO	24 AUGUST TO 23 SEPTEMBER	10	14	18	19	25	37	1	7	9	13
LIBRA	24 SEPTEMBER TO 23 OCTOBER	7	8	16	28	30	37	4	5	8	12
SCORPIO	24 OCTOBER TO 22 NOVEMBER	14	25	29	32	37	39	2	7	10	12
SAGITTARIUS	23 NOVEMBER TO 21 DECEMBER	4	8	22	26	30	32	4	6	9	13
CAPRICORN	22 DECEMBER TO 20 JANUARY	7	9	10	14	33	34	1	5	11	12
AQUARIUS	21 JANUARY TO 19 FEBRUARY	10	11	20	28	29	38	4	6	7	10
PISCES	20 FEBRUARY TO 20 MARCH	9	15	17	24	30	36	1	6	8	13

Your Lucky Lotto

The prevailing planetary influences are the basis for this astro-guide to lucky Lotto numbers in 2018. Any Lotto forecast must be fallible, but to give yourself the best chance of winning, refer to the section on your birth sign.

ARIES
BORN 21 MARCH TO 20 APRIL

'Do it right away' is your motto, being a creature of impulse and someone who loves the thrill of the gamble. As Uranus, the planet of inspiration and genius is still moving through your sign (for at least 6 months), you should follow any sudden intuitive feeling for a particular number. Alternatively, select numbers linked to joint bank accounts, tax/NI details, or medical matters, such as your GP's address or phone number.

2	4	12	13	19	22	23	28	41	44
7	8	15	16	23	27	32	35	49	53

TAURUS
BORN 21 APRIL TO 21 MAY

Brilliant, intuitive and unpredictable Uranus begins its passage through your sign in the second half of the year, shaking things up a little, no doubt. Go with unpredictability when it comes to your numbers and choose on a whim! This year, playing the lottery with a colleague may go well for Taurus as could selecting numbers connected to your spouse, partner or a life-long companion.

5	8	21	26	37	38	42	44	50	51
9	12	33	35	41	40	46	48	58	59

LEO
BORN 24 JULY TO 24 AUGUST

Leo likes a grand gesture and, as a Fire sign, you are given to impulse and intuition. This year, however, if you normally play the lottery haphazardly, try to stick to a new selection of favourite numbers for the whole year. For an additional tip, try digits associated with your home or your past, in particular anything you can think of from childhood or related to your parents, especially your father.

1	2	11	12	26	28	41	43	44	48
4	8	13	19	30	33	44	45	51	55

VIRGO
BORN 24 AUGUST TO 24 SEPTEMBER

Virgo, being a realistic Earth sign, rarely puts much faith in the unreliability of luck and chance, preferring tried-and-tested analysis and common sense planning. When it comes to playing the lottery this year, stick to the same numbers if you normally play that way; and if not, choose a new set and keep them. Otherwise, choose numbers connected to communications such as your phone, fax or even IP address.

2	3	11	14	28	35	42	44	50	52
8	9	22	26	37	38	46	49	56	58

SAGITTARIUS
BORN 24 NOVEMBER TO 21 DECEMBER

You are the optimistic risk-taker of the zodiac and are often blessed with good luck. This year, the astrological picture indicates a lot of change; don't bother to stick with favourite digits but instead go with the flow and chop and change your numbers on a whim as you move though 2018. Consider making some of the numbers you select related to your recent past, or to a hospital you may recently have visited.

1	4	11	14	31	33	40	42	51	53
5	6	24	25	35	37	47	49	58	59

CAPRICORN
BORN 25 DECEMBER to 20 JANUARY

Saturn, the planet of time, patience and consistency, is now in your sign so perhaps it's time to stay with one set of numbers. Saturn doesn't tend to bestow random luck, but that doesn't preclude you from playing with others in a pair, or a syndicate, to benefit from their good fortune! When choosing your numbers, go for those associated with a friend, social group or club you many belong to.

2	6	16	18	24	27	39	42	49	50
8	10	21	23	31	35	44	48	52	54

Astro-guide for 2018

Choose two numbers from the first square, then one number from each of the following squares. Either keep to the same numbers each week or vary the astrological indicators according to your personal vibrations.

USING THIS SYSTEM READER WINS **£40,000** MRS THERESE SINGER OF GLASGOW

GEMINI
BORN 25 MAY TO 21 JUNE

You are changeable and mercurial by temperament and you are advised to stay true to form when selecting your lottery numbers this year. Follow any strong hunches and let your dreams be a source of inspiration. Remember, your ruling planet Mercury brings the gift of prophecy and divination! An extra tip for a lottery win this year would be to choose numbers linked to your workplace, or a work colleague.

2	9		18	19		25	28		36	38		47	50
11	14		20	23		29	32		40	43		55	57

CANCER
BORN 25 JUNE TO 25 JULY

Old Man Saturn, Lord of Fate, is in your opposite sign for the next twelve months. This indicates that you should honour consistency and keep to the same numbers when playing the lottery. Stick with any favourite numbers for the whole twelve months. If you need to choose new numbers, consider those associated with a romantic partner, a place of leisure and entertainment or your children.

6	7		17	18		24	28		41	44		50	52
9	10		21	22		37	39		46	49		57	58

LIBRA
BORN 24 SEPTEMBER TO 24 OCTOBER

Eccentric Uranus is passing through your opposite sign of Aries this year, perhaps making life inconsistent for you at best. But with Jupiter, the planet of luck, in your solar second house of finance right now you may be seeing the benefits of new monetary opportunities. Your chart this year suggests you could be lucky by selecting numbers associated with personal finance, such as bank account numbers or sorting codes.

2	6		10	13		26	28		37	38		44	49
7	8		19	25		32	35		40	41		55	58

SCORPIO
24 OCTOBER TO 25 NOVEMBER

Spontaneity and a 'go with the flow' approach offer the best prospects of a win on the Lotto in 2018. This is because Jupiter, the planet of luck, now makes its presence felt in your sign. Choose your numbers apparently randomly and you may be being guided by something bigger! Alternatively, choose numbers are specific to you – height or weight, measurements, or your 'signature' in numerology.

1	2		11	19		25	28		36	37		49	53
7	8		20	22		30	34		46	48		54	59

AQUARIUS
BORN 21 JANUARY TO 19 FEBRUARY

You just might want to avoid the random approach this year, Aquarius. The astrological picture suggests you should be playing consistently: try to keep to your well-loved numbers and resist the temptation to alter them. As a guide to numbers themselves, your solar tenth house is accentuated, so try ones associated with your boss at work, your mother or anything at all to do with your career or profession.

5	9		16	19		29	32		40	41		54	55
11	14		22	23		34	39		43	48		57	58

PISCES
BORN 20 FEBRUARY TO 20 MARCH

Idealistic, dreamy and psychic Neptune continues through Pisces in 2018, so use the power of personal intuition on the Lotto. Make a dream diary and jot down any numbers that may appear in a dream. Also, your solar ninth house is accentuated, so you could select numbers connected to any recent long journeys, foreign holidays, higher education courses or even religious institutions you may have visited recently.

6	8		15	16		26	27		38	39		47	49
10	11		20	21		35	36		44	45		52	56

Euro Millions Astro-indicator for 2018

Twelve has always been the perfect 'cyclical' number and is the 'pool' from which you can select from numbers below – they may help to improve your chances. Find your sun sign in the left-hand column, then read across the first panel and choose five numbers (1–50) for the main board. Then, two for the Lucky Star section on the right. Some will overlap.

ARIES 21 March to 20 April	2	6	8	14	32	33	47	50	3	5	8	11
TAURUS 21 April to 21 May	1	5	22	28	29	33	35	46	2	3	4	6
GEMINI 22 May to 21 June	1	6	12	24	30	40	47	49	4	9	10	11
CANCER 22 June to 22 July	2	3	9	27	31	39	40	42	1	6	7	9
LEO 23 July to 23 August	1	11	15	23	27	42	46	48	3	6	9	12
VIRGO 24 August to 23 September	3	6	17	22	25	26	47	48	1	2	5	11
LIBRA 24 September to 23 October	4	13	20	22	35	37	39	49	1	3	4	12
SCORPIO 24 October to 22 November	2	4	15	28	32	40	41	45	6	9	10	11
SAGITTARIUS 23 November to 21 December	6	7	14	21	25	29	33	43	1	7	8	9
CAPRICORN 22 December to 20 January	1	2	8	13	27	29	40	41	4	5	6	11
AQUARIUS 21 January to 19 February	3	7	13	30	38	42	45	49	2	3	5	9
PISCES 20 February to 20 March	4	5	16	19	20	35	46	47	1	4	7	10

Health Lottery Astro-Guide for 2018

Health Lottery forecasts are based on the strength of Jupiter and planetary associations with the solar sixth house. These aspects are traditionally connected to health matters, whilst Jupiter signifies good luck generally. The numbers below may help to improve your chances at winning: just find your sun sign, then select three numbers 1–50 from the first panel. Then choose two from the second 1–30.

Sign	Dates	First panel (1–50)	Second panel (1–30)
ARIES	21 March to 20 April	5 9 22 33 39 48	1 8 18 23
TAURUS	21 April to 21 May	9 10 15 21 29 33	3 7 11 29
GEMINI	22 May to 21 June	2 14 30 31 45 46	10 12 22 27
CANCER	22 June to 22 July	10 28 34 35 42 47	12 19 21 24
LEO	23 July to 23 August	1 16 20 34 40 43	5 6 19 29
VIRGO	24 August to 23 September	8 9 31 34 43 44	16 20 23 24
LIBRA	24 September to 23 October	2 7 14 33 41 46	15 19 26 27
SCORPIO	24 October to 22 November	14 19 28 37 44 46	5 7 12 27
SAGITTARIUS	23 November to 21 December	6 8 17 28 32 45	1 2 23 24
CAPRICORN	22 December to 20 January	21 30 37 39 43 48	10 16 23 24
AQUARIUS	21 January to 19 February	11 13 25 38 42 47	8 14 17 21
PISCES	20 February to 20 March	9 31 36 37 43 49	16 18 20 25

UK Fairs and Events 2018

*Dates may be based on traditional fixtures and both dates and venues are subject to change.
Always check local press or with organisers well in advance.*

AGRICULTURAL AND COUNTRYSIDE

Anglesey County Show: Gwalchmai 14–15 August
Appleby Horse Fair: Appleby-in-Westmorland, Cumbria 7–13 June
Autumn Show and Game Fair: South of England Centre, Ardingly, Haywards Heath 6–7 October
Bakewell Show: 1–2 August
Bingley Show: Myrtle Park, Bingley 21 July (provisional)
Black Isle Show: Mansfield Showground, Muir of Ord 2 August
Border Union Show: Springwood Park, Kelso 27–28 July
Cheshire County Show: Tabley, Nr Knutsford 19–20 June
Country Fest: Westmorland County Showground, Lane Farm, Crooklands, Milnthorpe 2–3 June
Countryside Live: Great Yorkshire Showground, Harrogate 20–21 October
Cumberland County Show: Rickerby Park, Carlisle 9 June
Denbigh and Flint Show: The Green, Denbigh 16 August
Derbyshire County Show: Elvaston, Nr Derby 23 June
Devon County Show: Westpoint, Clyst St Mary, Exeter 17–19 May
Dorset County Show: Dorchester Showground 1–2 September
Dumfries and Lockerbie Agricultural Show: Park Farm, Dumfries 4 August
East of England Autumn Show: Showground, Peterborough 14 October
East of England Show and Just Dogs Live: Showground, Peterborough 6–8 July
Edenbridge and Oxted Agricultural Show: Ardenrun Showground, Lingfield 27 August
Eye Show: Goodrich Park, Palgrave 26–27 August
Great Yorkshire Show: Great Yorkshire Showground, Harrogate 10–12 July
Hertfordshire County Show: The Showground, Redbourn 26–27 May
Kelso Ram Sales: Springwood Park 14 September
Kent County Show: Detling, Maidstone 6–8 July
Lincolnshire Show: Grange-de-Lings, Lincoln 21–22 June
Monmouthshire Show: Vauxhall Fields, Monmouth 30 August

Nantwich Show and International Cheese Awards: Dorfold Hall Park, Nantwich 25 July
New Forest and Hampshire County Show: New Park, Brockenhurst 24–26 July
Newark and Nottinghamshire County Show: Newark Showground, Newark-on-Trent 12–13 May
Newark Vintage Tractor and Heritage Show: Showground, Newark-on-Trent 10–11 November
North Somerset Show: Bathing Pond Fields, Wraxall, Nr Bristol 7 May
Northumberland County Show: Bywell, Nr Stocksfield 28 May
Oxfordshire County and Thame Show: Thame Showground 28 July
Pembrokeshire County Show: Withybush, Haverfordwest 21–23 August
Romsey Show: Broadlands, Romsey 8 September
Royal Bath & West Show: Showground, Shepton Mallet 30 May–2 June
Royal Bath & West AMES: Showground, Shepton Mallet 7 February
Royal Bath & West Dairy Show: Showground, Shepton Mallet 3 October
Royal Cornwall Show: Wadebridge 7–9 June
Royal County of Berkshire Show: Newbury Showground 15–16 September
Royal Highland Show: Ingliston, Edinburgh 21–24 June (provisional)
Royal Norfolk Show: Norfolk Showground, Norwich 27–28 June
Royal Welsh Show: Llanelwedd, Builth Wells 23–26 July
Royal Welsh Winter Fair: Llanelwedd, Builth Wells 26–27 November
Shire Horse Society Spring Show: Arena UK Showground, Allington 16–17 March
Shropshire County Show: West Midlands Agricultural Showground, Shrewsbury 19 May
South of England Show: South of England Centre, Ardingly, Haywards Heath 7–9 June
Staffordshire County Show: Stafford Showground 30–31 May
Suffolk Show: Trinity Park, Ipswich 30–31 May
Surrey County Show: Stoke Park, Guildford 28 May
Tendring Hundred Show: Lawford House Park, Nr Manningtree 14 July
Three Counties Show: Three Counties Showground, Malvern 15–17 June

Turriff Show: The Showground, Turriff,
  Aberdeenshire 4–5 Aug
Westmorland County Show: Lane Farm, Crooklands
  13 September

OTHER EVENTS

Badminton Horse Trials: 2–6 May
BBC Gardeners' World Live: NEC Birmingham
  14–17 June (provisional)
Blackpool Illuminations: 31 August–4 November
Border Union Championship Dog Show:
  Springwood Park, Kelso 16–17 June
Braemar Gathering: 1 September
Burghley Horse Trials: Burghley Park, Stamford
  30 August–2 September
Chester Folk Festival: Kelsall 28 May
Cowes Week: 4–11 August
Crufts Dog Show: NEC Birmingham 8–11 March
Edinburgh International Festival: 3–27 August
Edinburgh Military Tattoo: Edinburgh Castle
  Esplanade 3–25 August
Farnborough International Air Show: Farnborough
  Aerodrome 16–22 July
Gardening Scotland: Ingliston, Nr Edinburgh
  1–3 June
Golf. British Open Championship: Carnoustie
  19–22 July. Amateur: Royal Aberdeen & Murcar
  18–23 June. Boys Amateur: Royal Portrush &
  Portstewart 14–19 August. Seniors Amateur: Royal
  Porthcawl 1–3 August. Seniors Open: St Andrews
  26–29 July. Boys Home Internationals: Royal
  Dornoch 7–9 August. Junior Open: St Andrews
  16–18 July.
Hay Festival: Hay-on-Wye 24 May–3 June
Helston Furry Dance: 8 May
Henley Regatta: 4–8 July
The Hoppings (funfair): Town Moor, Newcastle
  22–30 June
Horse Racing. Cheltenham Gold Cup: 16 March.
  Grand National: Aintree 7 April. Scottish Grand
  National: Ayr 22 April. 2000 Guineas: Newmarket
  5 May (prov.). Epsom Derby: 2 June. Royal Ascot:
  19–23 June. Glorious Goodwood: 31 July–
  4 August (prov.). St Leger: Doncaster 8 September.
  King George VI Chase: Kempton 26 December.
Hull Fair: 5–13 October
Isle of Man TT Races: Douglas, IoM 26 May–8 June
Isle of Wight Festival: Seaclose Park, Newport, Isle
  of Wight 7–10 June
Jersey Battle of Flowers: 9 August
Llangollen International Musical Eisteddfod:
  10–15 July
London to Brighton Veteran Car Run: Hyde Park,
  London–Madeira Drive, Brighton 4 November
  (provisional)

London Harness Horse Parade: South of England
  Showground, Ardingly, Haywards Heath 2 April
London Marathon: Greenwich Park–The Mall,
  London 22 April
London Motor Show: Battersea Park 5–6 May
Lord Mayor's Show: City of London 10 November
Military Odyssey: Kent County Showground,
  Detling, Maidstone 25–27 August
Nottingham Goose Fair: 3–7 October (traditional
  fixture; check local press)
Notting Hill Carnival: 25–27 August
'Obby 'Oss Day (May Day): Padstow, 1 May
Oxford vs Cambridge Boat Race: River Thames,
  Putney–Mortlake 25 March
Ould Lammas Fair: Ballycastle 27–28 August
Palace to Place Cycle Ride: Buckingham Palace–
  Windsor Castle 30 September (provisional)
RHS Chelsea Flower Show: 22–26 May (RHS
  members only first two days. Advance booking
  required.)
RHS Flower Show: Bute Park, Cardiff 13–15 April
RHS Flower Show: Chatsworth Estate, Derbyshire
  6–10 June
RHS Flower Show: Tatton Park, Nr Knutsford,
  Cheshire 18–22 July
RHS Hampton Court Palace Flower Show: 4–9 July
  (RHS members only first two days. Advance
  booking required.)
RHS Malvern Autumn Show: Three Counties
  Showground 29–30 September
RHS Malvern Spring Show: Three Counties
  Showground 10–13 May
RideLondon: London–Surrey 29 July (provisional)
Royal International Air Tattoo: RAF Fairford,
  Gloucestershire 13–15 July
Royal Windsor Horse Show: Home Park, Windsor
  9–13 May
Shrewsbury Folk Festival: 24–27 August
Shropshire County Horse Show: West Midlands
  Agricultural Showground, Shrewsbury 19 May
Sidmouth Folk Week: 3–10 August
Tall Ships Regatta: Liverpool 25–28 May
Trooping the Colour: Horse Guards Parade, London
  16 June
Three Choirs Festival: Hereford 28 July–4 August
Three Counties Championship Dog Show: Malvern
  Showground, Malvern 7–10 June
Up Helly Aa (fire festival and torchlight parade):
  Lerwick, Shetland Isles 25 January
V Festival: Hylands Park, Chelmsford/Weston Park,
  South Staffs 18–19 August
Whitby Folk Festival: 25–31 August
Wimbledon Lawn Tennis Championships:
  27 June–10 July

Lighting-up Times for 2018

Vehicle lamps must be used between sunset and sunrise. Times are in GMT, except 01.00 on 25 March to 01.00 on 28 October when they are BST (1 hour in advance). They are calculated for London (longitude 0º, latitude N.51º5).

Day	January h m	February h m	March h m	April h m	May h m	June h m	July h m	August h m	September h m	October h m	November h m	December h m
1	16 32	17 19	18 10	20 03	20 53	21 38	21 50	21 18	20 17	19 08	17 03	16 25
2	16 33	17 21	18 12	20 05	20 55	21 39	21 50	21 16	20 14	19 06	17 01	16 24
3	16 34	17 23	18 14	20 06	20 56	21 40	21 50	21 15	20 12	19 03	17 00	16 23
4	16 35	17 25	18 15	20 08	20 58	21 41	21 49	21 13	20 10	19 01	16 58	16 23
5	16 36	17 27	18 17	20 10	21 00	21 42	21 49	21 11	20 08	18 59	16 56	16 22
6	16 37	17 28	18 19	20 11	21 01	21 43	21 48	21 10	20 05	18 57	16 54	16 22
7	16 39	17 30	18 21	20 13	21 03	21 44	21 47	21 08	20 03	18 54	16 53	16 22
8	16 40	17 32	18 22	20 15	21 04	21 44	21 47	21 06	20 01	18 52	16 51	16 21
9	16 41	17 34	18 24	20 16	21 06	21 45	21 46	21 04	19 59	18 50	16 50	16 21
10	16 43	17 36	18 26	20 18	21 08	21 46	21 45	21 02	19 56	18 48	16 48	16 21
11	16 44	17 38	18 28	20 20	21 09	21 47	21 45	21 00	19 54	18 46	16 47	16 21
12	16 46	17 49	18 29	20 22	21 11	21 47	21 44	20 58	19 52	18 43	16 45	16 21
13	16 47	17 41	18 31	20 23	21 12	21 48	21 43	20 57	19 49	18 41	16 44	16 21
14	16 49	17 43	18 33	20 25	21 14	21 48	21 42	20 55	19 47	18 39	16 42	16 21
15	16 50	17 45	18 34	20 27	21 15	21 49	21 41	20 53	19 45	18 37	16 41	16 21
16	16 52	17 47	18 36	20 28	21 17	21 49	21 40	20 51	19 42	18 35	16 39	16 21
17	16 53	17 49	18 38	20 30	21 18	21 50	21 39	20 49	19 40	18 33	16 38	16 21
18	16 55	17 50	18 40	20 32	21 20	21 50	21 38	20 47	19 38	18 31	16 37	16 22
19	16 57	17 52	18 41	20 33	21 21	21 50	21 37	20 45	19 36	18 29	16 36	16 22
20	16 58	17 54	18 43	20 35	21 23	21 51	21 35	20 42	19 33	18 26	16 34	16 22
21	17 00	17 56	18 45	20 37	21 24	21 51	21 34	20 40	19 31	18 24	16 33	16 23
22	17 02	17 58	18 46	20 38	21 25	21 51	21 33	20 38	19 29	18 22	16 32	16 23
23	17 03	17:59	18 48	20 40	21 27	21 51	21 32	20 36	19 26	18 20	16 31	16 24
24	17 05	18 01	18 50	20 42	21 28	21 51	21 30	20 34	19 24	18 18	16 30	16 25
25	17 07	18 03	19 51	20 43	21 29	21 51	21 29	20 32	19 22	18 16	16 29	16 25
26	17 09	18 05	19 53	20 45	21 31	21 51	21 27	20 30	19 19	18 14	16 28	16 26
27	17 10	18 07	19 55	20 47	21 32	21 51	21 26	20 28	19 17	18 12	16 27	16 27
28	17 12	18 08	19 56	20 48	21 33	21 51	21 24	20 25	19 15	18 11	16 27	16 28
29	17 14		19 58	20 50	21 34	21 51	21 23	20 23	19 13	17 09	16 26	16 28
30	17 16		20 00	20 51	21 35	21 51	21 21	20 21	19 10	17 07	16 25	16 29
31	17 18		20 01		21 37		21 20	20 19		17 05		16 30